Stephanie Vigil   Colle

REPUTATION
by Design

#image

Kendall Hunt
publishing company

Cover image supplied by Amanda Ford.

Kendall Hunt
publishing company

www.kendallhunt.com
Send all inquiries to:
4050 Westmark Drive
Dubuque, IA 52004-1840

Copyright © 2019 by Kendall Hunt Publishing Company

ISBN 978-1-5249-8731-2

Published in the United States of America

Brief Contents

Preface   ix

Acknowledgments   xi

About the Authors   xiii

Chapter 1   The Value of Your Reputation   1

Chapter 2   7 Seconds   11

Chapter 3   Show Us Your Selfie   19

Chapter 4   You Are What You Tweet   39

Chapter 5   Repairing Your Reputation   57

Chapter 6   Dis(Connect)   67

Chapter 7   Thank You!   73

Chapter 8   Say What???   81

Chapter 9   Success Starts Here   95

Chapter 10   Final Thoughts   107

Index   109

Contents

Preface ix

Acknowledgments xi

About the Authors xiii

Chapter 1: The Value of Your Reputation 1

It Is Not About the Money 1

But Can You Be Trusted? 2

Better to Be a People Magnet 3

Consistent People Are Dependable People 3

Gossip: Reputation Wrecker 4

Protect Your Assets 4

Authentically You! 5

Living With Integrity 7

Ramp Up Your Reputation 9

Chapter 2: 7 Seconds 11

There Is Always a First 12

Before You Even Open Your Mouth... 12

Attitude Is Everything 13

Can I Have a Do-Over? 16

Chapter 3: Show Us Your Selfie 19

Where Does Our Self-Image Come From? 20

Turning a Negative Into a Positive 23

Begin by Standing Up for What You Believe In 23

Learn to Lead With Love 23

Practice Forgiveness 23

Hurt People, Hurt People 24

When Is It Okay Not to Care What Others Think About Us? 24

Self-Esteem 25

What Is Holding Us Back? 25

Positive Reinforcement Goes a Long Way 26

CONTENTS

Developing a Healthy Self-Esteem   27
The Core of Me   28

Chapter 4: You Are What You Tweet   **39**
Social Media Is a Big, Glaring Spotlight on YOU!   39
Golden Rule   40
Social Media Can Be Fun!   42
Many People Have Secured Jobs Using Social Media   42
Like ME!!   43
Lonely and Depressed? You Are Not Alone   46
Anxiety   46
Bad Sleeping Habits   46
Communication Issues   46
Depression   47

Chapter 5: Repairing Your Reputation   **57**
The Comeback Kid   59
Formula for Success   63
Apologize and Be Authentic   63
Behave   64
Come Clean and Commit to Change   64
Deliberately Move Forward   64
Activity for Repairing Your Reputation   65
If I Could Have a "Do-Over"   65

Chapter 6: Dis(Connect)   **67**
No Time, No Problem   68
When Passion Meets Purpose   69
Volunteer to Make a Difference   69

Chapter 7: Thank You!   **73**
A Simple Note Can Change Your Life!   73
Stand Out From the Rest!   73
Is an E-Mail or Text Ok?   74
When Should I Write a Thank You?   74

CONTENTS

Personalize Your Message 74
   Only for You! 75
You Never Climb the Ladder Alone 75
Where Do I Start? 76

Chapter 8: Say What??? **81**
Active Listening 81
Speaking Successfully 82
Public Speaking 83
Preparation Is Key 84
Getting It Write 84
You Can Never Erase the Written Word 87
Do Not Let Lazy Be Your Excuse 87

Chapter 9: Success Starts Here **95**
Fear and Doubt 97
Accountability Is Key 97
Be Flexible 98
Track Your Progress 98
Let Us Put a Plan Together! 98

Chapter 10: Final Thoughts **107**

Index 109

Preface

Whom do you admire most in your life and why? This is the first question I ask my students at Gonzaga University upon getting to know them. Their answers usually use words like these: *trustworthy, dependable, a good listener, positive, hardworking, genuine, loving, motivated, never gives up despite their circumstances.*

In all my years of teaching Image & Reputation management, never once have I heard them say, *"I admire this person for the amount of money he makes."*

Can you imagine someone standing up and using all those wonderful words to describe you? Admiration usually happens because a person has been deliberate with his or her actions and intentional with his or her words. Not just to one person but to many throughout his or her lifetime. It is the way they live their lives that is so respectable. Time and time again they show you they can be trusted and would drop most things when you need them. These traits are rare these days, but they do not have to be. Developing healthy habits early can set you up for success in countless ways. Many of the students who have taken this class have seen rewarding results just by learning more about themselves.

"I think that was the most applicable class I have ever taken in my life."

This book is based on a course that Stephanie Vigil has been teaching on the undergraduate and graduate level at Gonzaga University for several years. The course is unique and it is not offered anywhere else. Students who have taken the class highly recommend that *every* undergraduate should be exposed to these concepts. They wish they had been encouraged to pay attention to their image and reputation in high school. *Reputation by Design* is not solely intended for use in the classroom. We do not want this book to feel like a "textbook," per se, rather a useful resource that you will come back to over and over for helpful tips and ideas for self-reflection that will assist you in presenting your *best self* as you journey through the many changes in your life.

It is useful for anyone from high school students to college students, professionals, parents, or anyone at any point in their lives looking to enhance their image and reputation. Do not wait until you are college-aged to start setting yourself up for success! And if you are a professional, it is never too late to "look in the mirror" and see what you would like to do to enhance your own reputation.

Our students convinced us that we needed to spread the word to a broader audience.

"This class taught me how my appearance can make an immediate impression on someone and how necessary it is to manage your social media accounts in this digital age."

"In all, when Prof. Vigil reminded us that 'your reputation and image are in your control' I really understood what she meant. So much of what I learned today are things that I can control in my life. I now understand that I need to find the balance of sharing and connecting with others on social media, and maintaining the professional image that I would like companies and co-workers to see me as."

"The exercises and discussions we had in class helped us shape our view of ourselves, our brand, reputation, first impressions, and so much more. I hope everyone in the class benefited from it as much as I did, and I genuinely hope more students get the opportunity to experience this class."

"Now I'll never forget to write a thank you note!!!"

We often get caught up in the moment and can forget that anything we say or do on the Internet is not private. As the world continues to use more and more technology, we must stop to think about our actions and ensure that we are not going to do something we will later regret. Our reputation and image are important pieces of us that once broken are not easily fixed. You can spend years building a reputation, but it takes seconds to ruin it.

"This course gave me a lot of insight in to how quickly one's image can be destroyed, but also how to take precautionary measures to make sure that doesn't happen and how to overcome it if it does. Learning that it would take approximately three and a half years to regain my reputation if I were to fall from grace really motivates me to value my image more than I have and to make sure that I focus on the things that are important in my life and to not lose sight of that."

In an era where social media monopolizes people's time, education on image and reputation is absolutely crucial. From politicians to athletes to corporate leaders, it seems that new people pop up in the news every day having done something to damage their reputation or the reputation of their organization. If we can learn from other people's mistakes and the steps they have taken to repair their reputation, perhaps others will learn how to avoid these mistakes in the first place.

We are confident that by the time you finish reading, this book will make you think about how you are portraying yourself, both personally and digitally. This book is intended to teach you new habits and give you a formula for success while creating a *Reputation by Design*.

© Artur Szczybylo/Shutterstock.com

Acknowledgments

A large number of people have contributed to the completion of this book.

We never would have completed this book without our Saturday mornings fueled by Revel 77 Coffee in Spokane.

Our incredibly supportive spouses put up with our dueling computers and editing sessions over speakerphone as well as many hours away from family.

We are extremely grateful to all the friends and professionals who provided testimonials and quotes included in this book.

Amber, our cover photographer took our idea and made it come to life! And of course, we could not have had the successful photo shoot without our enthusiastic models: Amy, Johnathan, and Amina.

© sripfoto/Shutterstock.com

We want to thank family and friends who not only provided ideas and feedback for our book content, but also those who read sample chapters and provided suggestions and confirmation.

Finally, we would be remiss if we didn't acknowledge our team of "enforcers" at Kendall Hunt, Bev Kraus and Meghan Edwards. They kept us on task, following the rules, and able to meet our deadline. And we need to express our gratitude to Lara McCombie, also of Kendall Hunt, for encouraging us to write this book.

About the Authors

Colleen is on left, and Stephanie is on right

Stephanie has been an award-winning journalist for the past 25 years. She has worked for KHQ TV (the local NBC affiliate) for more than two decades with her same co-anchor, Dan Kleckner. She received her master's degree in communication and leadership at Gonzaga University in 2013 and began teaching a course she designed for the School of Business called *Image and Reputation*—the inspiration for this book.

Stephanie and her husband, Jay, share five children and one grandchild together.

Stephanie has competed in the 70.3 Ironman, half-marathons, and triathlons. She loves crossing finish lines, cycling, learning, traveling, boating and enjoying time with family and friends.

Colleen has been a professor at Gonzaga University for 33 years, specializing in advanced public speaking, organizational and interpersonal communication, writing for public relations, and public relations research. She also served as associate dean for the College of Arts & Sciences for the better part of 17 years. She received her master's degree in organizational communication from Washington State University in 1984. She has been the co-author of three communication and public speaking textbooks prior to the writing of this book. She serves as a public speaking coach and communication consultant.

Colleen and her husband, Mike, have been married for 32 years. Together they have two children: Maureen (husband Chad) and Colin, and two grandchildren.

She enjoys time with her family and grandchildren, golf, cooking, and traveling to warm climates (in search of beaches and golf courses). She also practices yoga and appreciates outdoor power walks.

chapter 1

THE VALUE OF YOUR REPUTATION

Value your reputation like it is your most precious commodity. It could mean the difference between landing a job, losing one, or never getting a single glance. Most of us know that it takes time

"You can't buy a reputation; you must earn it."
—Harvey Mackay

and effort to build a good reputation, and it can be gone in no time. If you think about it, whether you are sizing people up either personally or professionally, you screen them based on their reputation. If it is your intention to *design* your reputation, why not make it a masterpiece?

It Is Not About the Money

The masterpiece is YOU, not your possessions. "Success is how you look at yourself. It's not measured by money, status or property," says Patricia McRae, President, KHQ Inc. & Cowles Montana Media. Money can buy you objects and experiences, but it cannot buy you what should be most important in life. If you are motivated only by money, you will find yourself greatly disappointed. The things that people desire like love, respect, and trust must be earned. We have met some very rich people in our lives that are absolutely miserable because they did not work on the intangibles that cannot be bought.

Most people who see themselves as hard working, respectful, and trustworthy are often those with a valued reputation. "For me, image is about authenticity. Authenticity, hard

MONEY DOESN'T MAKE YOU HAPPY

work, and being a good person will create a reputation you can be proud of. Image, like anything in life, is about the decisions you make and how hard you want to work," says Chris Indelicato, CEO/President of Delicato Family Vineyards, one of the fastest growing wine companies in the world. People who work hard at achieving a great reputation oftentimes reap large financial rewards. They become a commodity because they stand out from the pack. Success is their reward.

But Can You Be Trusted?

If you cannot be trusted you will not succeed. People will not want to hang around you, do business with you, or associate themselves with you. When an untrustworthy person hurts us, we know how far we distance ourselves from him or her after that. Trust is sacred, but also scarce these days. If you are a trustworthy person, expect great things to happen to you. We like the way Bonnie Quinn, President/Owner of QUINN Advertising puts it:

© Gustavo Frazao/Shutterstock.com

"There has never been a more urgent time to achieve TRUST in our public image.

T – Truth: Am I honest? Do I speak the same in person, on social media and behind closed doors?

R – Respect: Am I respectful to all people?

U – Unity: Does my communication aspire to bring people together for common goal?

S – Service: Do I consider the needs of others as part of my life's goals?

T – Transparency: Being a trustworthy person requires some level of risk; I must demonstrate some level of transparency and vulnerability."

Bonnie Quinn Clausen
President/Owner QUINN Advertising

Do those words describe you? Others want to associate with people who possess these qualities. Trust is broken every day, but it does not have to be . . . not by YOU!

Better to Be a People Magnet

People gravitate toward those they admire. A proficient manager will have a long list of contacts because of his or her great reputation. This will allow him or her to attract the strongest candidates on the job market. This is also the reason why you should strive to maintain, or even strengthen an already healthy reputation. "When you naturally put the requests and desires of others before your own, you just inherently build loyalty, trust, competency, and accountability that puts you on the road to a good but more likely a great reputation where it matters most," states

© APTX4869/Shutterstock.com

Linda Underwood, U.S. Bank President. If the public perceives you as having a good reputation, they are more likely to come to your defense should your character be questioned. A well-respected reputation reaps many rewards.

Consistent People Are Dependable People

© marekuliasz/Shutterstock.com

One of the keys to gaining and maintaining a solid reputation is consistency; consistency in both your words and actions. Repetition makes reputation. People will come to expect you to act with integrity and authenticity because you consistently do so. How does this translate into action? For one, it means taking your commitments seriously. If you say "yes" to something, commit to that "yes" and make sure you follow through. And do not say "yes" if you do not really mean it. It is hard for some of us to say "no," but we act with more integrity if we do. We say things like, "I'll think about it," or "I'll look into it," sometimes believing that we actually will, but in reality, often we are simply postponing a decision or softening a "no." But we are not being honest, even if we have well-meaning intentions. As Henry Ford said, "You can't build a reputation on what you're going to do."

Amy Elisa Jackson wrote for Glassdoor in 2017, "Making up an excuse or a fake set of circumstances to get you out of the work makes you look bad." (Jackson, 2017) Provide a thoughtful and honest explanation and you will be more respected in the long run. Taking on responsibilities is one way to build your reputation, as long as you can follow through.

Gossip: Reputation Wrecker

Most of us grew up hearing our parents say, over and over, "If you can't say anything nice, don't say anything at all." People with stellar reputations continue to live by that motto. You do not hear them saying negative things about others. This is easier said than done, but we guarantee you will be far more successful and enjoy a much better reputation if you give up the negative talk.

How do you respond when a friend denigrates someone else? Do you chime in? Do you stay silent? How you respond says a lot about your character. No one ever looks good trying to make someone else look bad. What if you redirected the conversation or politely challenged the other person to look for the good in others? Set an example for others and success will follow. Would you not like to have a reputation of being that person who never says anything bad about others?

Think about the people in this world whom you trust, admire, and respect. What is it about them that makes you respect them? What are their qualities and characteristics? Maybe you have told yourself that you would really like to be more like them. When you imagine how they might behave in a particular situation, copy their behavior, and soon you will find that it becomes second nature to you.

Protect Your Assets

Treat your words and actions as a part of your personal brand. While you may feel that what you say now will not harm you, it may come back to haunt you in the future and can result in devastating consequences. As reported in Ed Tech Review, "A survey done by the Denver Post uncovered that 75% of U.S. adults that Googled themselves said their search results were NOT positive." ("Your digital footprint: Online reputation breakdown") Political comments, anything hurtful or biased with regard to race, gender, or sexual orientation, and questionable photos, are all examples of the types of posts that can be resurrected in the future and be used against you. Remember, you only have one reputation. Nurture it and care for it, starting right now.

Your reputation is always on the line. You need to consistently prove that you are worthy of respect. Strive to live your life in such a way that if someone were to speak poorly about you, no one would believe it.

Authentically You!

Remember, a good reputation is not an end goal; rather, it is a motivation to continue to be the person you most want to be. Be a role model for others. Two key traits of successful people who enjoy great reputations are authenticity and integrity. Let us talk about that.

So many wonderful things become possible when we have the courage to tell the truth, be ourselves, and live with real authenticity. Your offline life should match your online life. If it does not, trust disappears, your dependability erodes, opportunities dissolve, flaws appear in your character, and relationships disappear.

© Gustavo Frazao/Shutterstock.com

"Your inner brand has to match your online brand. It is very important to combine them both. Be who you are in your personal life and be who you are in your professional life. Then make sure these fit together online. As technology and social media continue to grow, there has never been before such importance around transparency, which means showing who you really are." ("The power of first impressions online")

> "Be yourself, everyone else is taken."—Oscar Wilde

Do not try to be someone you are not. Authenticity is about being *you,* fully. It is about realness and genuineness. When we are authentic we are vulnerable, aware, open, curious, and truthful above all else.

What are some of the benefits of authenticity? You will increase your self-confidence and willingness to pursue your passions. You will have the freedom to distance yourself from the things that hold you back—things like worry, excuses,

> "Vulnerability is not weakness," —Brene Brown

opinions, avoidance, and manipulation. You will have enhanced connections with yourself and others. In turn, you will have peace of mind, fun, self-acceptance, self-appreciation, and self-love.

The good news is that you do not have to be perfect! We all have imperfections and know how valuable it can be to learn from our mistakes. And in showing how we can learn from our mistakes we can help other people do the same.

Award winning journalist, Alex Rozier is well respected by his family, colleagues, and friends.

By looking at him you would never know something was wrong. His career was taking off; he had an overabundance of friends. He seemingly had it all, but his "secret" was keeping him from living his life to the fullest.

Source: Blake Rozier

"For a guy who speaks professionally for a living you would think I'd be smooth in a situation like this . . . but I'll be honest . . . . I struggled to find the words. I don't remember the exact quote, but I know I looked directly at the three of them and said something like this . . .

'Every single day of my life . . . every day . . . I work as hard as possible with one goal in mind . . . I just want to make you three proud. That's all I've ever wanted. That's it. But I'm hurting . . . hurting badly . . . and I need you to know my truth.

Mom, Dad, Blake . . . I'm gay.'"

Terrified he would hurt the ones he loved most he kept his secret for a very long time.

"I won't get into the specifics of what my family told me that night, but I will share a few of my mom's words:

'All I ever want is for my boys to be happy.'

Talk about unconditional love . . . wow.

My family loved me in that moment and they love me today.

I am so grateful. So relieved.

I wish I wouldn't have waited, but when I look back I wouldn't change a thing. My experience shaped my character. And now I've never been happier, knowing with certainty exactly who I am."

> "The core of authenticity is the courage to be imperfect, vulnerable, and to set boundaries."—Brené Brown

The love and support Alex received after sharing his sexuality with the world overwhelmed him. He was afraid of others judging him and worried about the toll it would take on his career. That was not the case. Alex is respected and trusted by many. Just recently he was promoted by his company and moved to the fifth largest city in the nation, Dallas, TX, where he continues to live out his dream as an award-winning journalist.

It takes courage to be vulnerable. Authentic people do not make excuses for who they are. They come to the table, flaws and all, and are perfectly comfortable in their own skin.

When you have a solid reputation you will be described as "authentic." You will also be a person of great integrity.

Living With Integrity

Integrity is one of the most, if not *the most,* important principle of leadership. Trust and honesty are central to integrity. It means telling the truth even when telling the truth is not easy or convenient. It is the most important piece of the puzzle that is often missing.

A person of integrity is reliable and can be counted on to do the right thing. You can count on that person to behave consistently in all aspects of his or her life, even if no one is watching or if it is not the easiest route to take.

We have all found ourselves in situations where the easiest thing to do is to ignore something or pretend you do not know about something when you actually do. The *easy* route is to let someone else deal with it or take responsibility. But the person of integrity takes responsibility and communicates truthfully, even when it may not feel good to do so.

When you act with integrity you are living your values and morals in all your relationships, both personal and professional. You keep your word and your commitments. You take responsibility for your

© Tashatuvango/Shutterstock.com

actions even when it would be easy to blame someone else. You demonstrate respect in all that you do and say. Sounds like a pretty steep challenge for sure, but if you behave consistently and with intention, you will establish a reputation of being a person of integrity.

When you have integrity, people know they can trust and depend on you, and there is a direct impact on your success in life. And remember, that even though you want to live your life with integrity, you also want to remain humble.

Unfortunately, all too often you hear stories of people whose actions demonstrate a clear *lack* of integrity. Just turn on the news. How often do you read stories about people making the right choices? Why not be the designer of your own reputation as a person of integrity? There are no downsides, only upsides.

Bottom line: People who value themselves rarely sell themselves short. They know the biggest investment they can make in life is in themselves. Your stock rises when people see you as a consistently dependable person with good moral character. To be authentic is to be 100% you with no regrets. Use your thoughts, actions and words to create a ***Reputation by Design***.

Ramp Up Your Reputation

We have talked a lot in this chapter about the importance and value of your reputation. As you finish reading this chapter, ponder this question: What is your reputation worth to you? Do you know how you would answer that question? Interview two people that you believe are not only successful, but also enjoy a very strong (positive) reputation in their community. Ask them what their reputation is worth to them, and what steps they have taken to ensure that they keep a solid reputation. Then, compare the responses from the two interviews. Are there some common threads and similarities? If so, what are they? What are some of the unique responses you received from the two different interviews?

Reflect on the responses that you received in the interviews. In the space below, describe the things you learned that will inspire you to continue to strive to develop and maintain a solid reputation. If you are doing this exercise as part of a class, share your findings with a partner or small group and compare your results.

_____

_____

_____

_____

_____

_____

_____

_____

_____

_____

_____

_____

_____

_____

_____

_____

_____

References

Jackson, A. E. (2017, January 19). *3 polite ways to turn down extra work*. Retrieved from https://www .glassdoor.com/blog/3-polite-ways-to-turn-down-extra-work

The power of first impressions online. (n.d.). Retrieved from http://www.marginalia.online/ the-power-of-first-impressions-online

Your digital footprint: Online reputation breakdown. (2015, May 19). Retrieved from https://wersm .com/your-digital-footprint-online-reputation-breakdown

chapter 2

7 SECONDS

It is not a coincidence that you meet people for the very first time and immediately decide whether or not you like them. They may not even speak a word, but you have already sized them up in your mind. You have decided whether or not they can be trusted or whether they will fit into your group or organization. You decide whether or not the person is competent, likable, motivated, or the right person to date, hire, promote, or do business with. First impressions can open doors for you both personally and professionally if you know how to do it right!

> "You never get a second chance to make a first impression."
> —Andrew Grant

A simple 7 second rush to judgment will confirm what *you* believe you already know based on your existing beliefs, past experiences, or theories. Chances are slim you will give that person a second chance to change your mind. Researchers refer to this as confirmation bias. You do not look at people objectively; instead, you make assumptions about who they are because of what you see, not what you know. The problem with confirmation bias is that it is one-sided, it can lead to errors, and cause people to jump to conclusions. But while you cannot control the thoughts of others, you can be aware that this bias is constantly happening and you can ask yourselves this question: How do I want others to see me? Answering this question allows you to create a *Reputation by Design.* Designing a first impression begins with intention and self-awareness.

There Is Always a First

Picture yourself getting ready for a first date. You are excited! Perhaps you are a little nervous. You want to look and feel your best. You make sure your hair looks good, your breath smells good, and your smile is on just right. You walk to the closet and pick out something that looks nice on you. You usually pick a color that you like. You want your clothes to fit well and be comfortable to wear. At first glance you want this person to be excited and to get to know you better.

Now apply this feeling to almost everything you do.

Whether you are on a first date, first day of school, or first job interview, you will want to do the same thing. Tailor your outfit to the setting you will be in, but ultimately strive to look and feel your best when you are trying to impress someone.

Many believe 7 seconds is an outdated number when it comes to making a first impression. Some studies suggest you can now be sized up in less than a second. This could be that we are exercising confirmation bias quicker these days because of social media. We click, swipe, like, and scroll through our pages faster than ever. We all like to say, "Don't judge me." But realistically that is what is happening every second of the day.

Before You Even Open Your Mouth…

Your appearance and behavior are two of the first things people will notice.

Have you ever judged a person just by looking at the lines on his or her face? Our emotions eventually show up on our faces. Smile lines, also known as Crow's Feet indicate a joyful person.

Frown lines can suggest you are a worrier, or think *too* much. People who grind their teeth or clench their jaws can look tense. Pursing your lips can suggest anger or bitterness. These are just a few things people instantly notice.

© Tetiana Tychynska/ Shutterstock.com

© Syda Productions/Shutterstock.com

They will also notice the way you dress. Your clothes say a lot about you. If you are going on a job interview, you will want to make sure your suit is tailored to fit you just right. We believe you should stick with a traditional suit regardless of the company you are interviewing with. It is best to play it safe. Fit into the culture of the (company/ employer) once you have been hired.

Remember, too, that people will be paying attention not only to your clothes, but also how you accessorize what you are wearing. Jewelry, watches, shoes, make-up, and hair are all sized up when making first impressions. Make sure that all these items send the message that you intend.

People also notice your body language. Tapping your foot or shaking a knee makes you appear less confident. Biting your nails makes you look nervous. People crossing their arms or legs, or both, can be seen as defensive or closed up. Leaning in shows that you are interested, leaning back means the opposite. We look for these nonverbal cues that will tell us how to proceed.

© Antonio Guillem/Shutterstock.com

Attitude Is Everything

We always know when students are engaged. It shows on their faces. They smile. They look at us. They may nod their heads. They will come prepared and engage in conversation.

Conversely, we know when they are not engaged. They may look stressed. They oftentimes look down and they do not raise their hands. Their arms are usually crossed. They could be slouched at their desks and we know that we are not going to be getting through to them that day. They do not want to receive our message. Facial expressions, body language, and behavior say so much without a word coming out of their mouths.

Have you ever tried having a conversation with people while they are staring at their phones? They might call themselves good multitaskers, but the receiver sees something different. The perception is that you are just not interested, or you have better things to do. The best impression you can make is to keep your phone out of sight. Check it when your time with them has ended. Give them the courtesy of your attention. You can develop a great reputation by exercising the art of active listening just by putting your phone away.

Ditch your phone—Hard to do, but so very important!
Be on Time! You risk any opportunity you may have by showing up late. Allow extra time to get where you need to be.
Dress for Success—People who look good feel good. They have a confidence that shines from the inside out. Find a suit or outfit that you absolutely love and wear it.

Good Eye Contact—If your eyes are the window to your soul, let them see who you are.

Make eye contact at least 75% of the time.

Firm Handshake—Practice this on a friend. A firm handshake, but not too hard, is a sign of mutual respect. It sets the tone for your time together.

Great Smile—Everyone loves a nice smile. It shows your kindness and appreciation. Smile, and approach new people with a genuine interest in getting to know them.

© kalen/Shutterstock.com

© mimagephotography/ Shutterstock.com

Posture—Good postures shows that you are present, engaged, and confident.

Gestures—Indicate you are very much a part of this conversation and enjoying yourself.

Stories up your sleeve—Everyone loves a good story.

Show Enthusiasm—Show interest in others, and be interesting yourself. People can tell if you are genuinely interested in getting to know them. That may start with making sure you remember their names.

A future _____ (You insert word; boyfriend? Girlfriend? Employer?) will want you around. Enthusiasm is contagious energy.

Say my name—Regardless of how difficult it may be for you to remember names, it should be a top priority for you. Studies show that just by hearing your name, even in a noisy setting, your brain is triggered. Remembering a person's name enhances your credibility. Best-selling author, Keith Ferrazzi, says that your first real step toward remembering names is to make the decision to care. "If you make a conscious decision that you are going to remember names," he explains, "because you care about the people you meet, you will immediately become much better at doing it!"(Hedges, 2013)

Another well-known tip, but worth the reminder, is to repeat the person's name that you have just met a few times during your initial conversation. "Oh, hello Lexi, it's so nice to meet you. This is the first time I am coming to this yoga class. How long have you been practicing here, Lexi?" By starting the conversation saying the person's name and repeating his or her name at the end of a question or statement a few times during that initial conversation, you increase your chances of remembering the name.

You may be thinking there is no way someone sizes all this up in a mere 7 seconds, but they do. We are observant creatures.

Can I Have a Do-Over?

First impressions cannot have do-overs, but they do evolve over time, and you can take steps to correct a bad one. Let us face it. Most of you can probably recall a time when you got off on the wrong foot with someone through your own fault or due to a circumstance beyond your control. Either way, the first impression you gave was not the one you had hoped for. Maybe you got stuck in traffic, forgot to add something to your calendar (or got the time or day wrong), a family emergency arose, you name it—life happens and you missed a meeting.

Keep in mind that each following meeting with someone allows you the opportunity to influence the other person's impression of you. More often than not, the initial impression is not set in stone. It may feel like it is a little sticky, but it is still moveable if you make the effort.

Recognize that shifting someone's perception of you will take time. One Harvard study quantifies this by suggesting that it takes eight positive interactions to counteract the initial negative one.

While the "easiest" way to save face would be to make up an excuse, that is not the route we would recommend. A favorite boss of mine once told me, "Always tell the truth, and you never have to remember anything." Apologize up front, and do not try to shift the blame on anyone or anything.

Bottom line: Now that you have read the entire chapter, consider this....The 7 seconds may have already happened before you even had a chance to meet that person face to face. Your online reputation preceded you. Chances are very good that your name was Googled and your social media sites were viewed. Your first meeting is a chance to reaffirm what he thinks he already knows. Chances are he will be even more impressed because you are taking the time to create a **Reputation by Design**.

Reference

Hedges, K. (2013, August 21). *The five best tricks to remember names.* Retrieved from https://www.forbes.com/sites/work-in-progress/2013/08/21/the-best-five-tricks-to-remember-names

chapter 3

SHOW US YOUR SELFIE

© ayelet-keshet/Shutterstock.com

What do you *see* when you look in the mirror? Better yet, what do you *say* to the person you see? "Funny?" "Fat?" "Smart?" "Not good enough?" "Too big?" "Too short?"

Are the words you use to describe yourself helpful or harmful to your well-being?

Your self-image is the mental picture you, and others, have about your physical appearance. Do you see what could be wrong with this picture? We let *others*

> ## "Talk to yourself like you would to someone you love."
> ## —Brene Brown

© Suzanne Tucker/Shutterstock.com

define who we are, and the problem with that is that we are more likely to remember the critical comments more than the wonderful compliments.

Negative events and experiences are imprinted in our minds quicker and they often last longer than positive ones.

"Nastiness just makes a bigger impact on our brains." This is what psychologists call negativity bias. "Your brain is simply built with a greater sensitivity to unpleasant news." ("Our Brain's Negative Bias")

"For a multitude of reasons including biology and chemistry, we're more likely to register an insult or negative event than we are to take in a compliment or recall details of a happy event." ("The negativity bias: Why the bad stuff sticks and how to overcome it.")

"It's why social scientists have found that it takes five compliments to make up for one criticism.

© De Visu/Shutterstock.com

19

It's also why those who can overcome their negativity bias are not only happier people, but also more successful." A study by psychologist Susan Segerstrom revealed, ". . . that 10 years after graduation, law students who were optimistic earned an average of $32,667 more than their pessimistic peers." (Warrell, 2017)

Where Does Our Self-Image Come From?

Harry Hazel, author of *The Art of Talking to Yourself and Others*, notes, "The self-image that we carry around today has very little to do with how we actually look or how intelligent we are." A positive or negative self-image is not something you are born with.

It begins early in our lives as we start to receive messages of approval, affirmation, disapproval, or encouragement from significant people in our lives. As you grew older, you received messages from

peers, teachers, family members, and other acquaintances which continued to shape your self-image and self-esteem.

One hurtful sentence lasted a lifetime for Leslie Lowe, a TV weather forecaster and owner of Pure Barre. Decades later she recalls the day one person changed the way she looked at herself in the mirror.

Leslie's Struggle with Self-Image

Twelve was not kind to me. We had just moved to a new town; my parents were going through a divorce and my world, as I knew it, was falling apart. I desperately wanted to fit in and was willing to do whatever it took. I cut off my long hair, guilted my parents into buying me the "right" clothes, and I went along with things that I didn't agree with just to be accepted.

I remember one day in 7th grade right after a gymnastics meet, finally feeling like I was part of the "in crowd" as I sat in a big circle with one of my new girlfriends and all the cute boys in our class. We were all laughing and

talking when out of nowhere this friend says to me, "Your legs are so fat"! I was so embarrassed! Had I never noticed that my legs were so fat?

That was the beginning of a very long downhill spiral with my self-image. Years of seeing nothing but fat legs every time I looked in the mirror led to years of obsessing about my weight, an eating disorder, anxiety and self-loathing.

It's taken years to begin to look at myself differently and to be able to love myself for everything that makes me different.

What's funny is that I have forgotten many faces and names from my youth, but to this day I still remember hers.

"So much of the reflection that we see in the mirror is what others have told us about ourselves. Over the years our perception of who we are becomes muddied. You are too fat, too short, not smart enough, you didn't go to the right school, wear the right clothes, live in the perfect house, in the perfect neighborhood, didn't have the right car," Leslie reflects. "When we are young, and sometimes old, we let ourselves be surrounded by people whose opinions don't matter, but we listen to anyway, and with people who would rather see us fail, than succeed. We forget that that says more about them than it does about us.

Leslie is not alone in her thoughts. We have been paying attention to negative rather than positive information since the beginning of time. It was a way to alert our cave-dwelling ancestors of danger.

Source: Nichole Mischke

Our past traumas have an effect on our lives and the way we deal with them. There is no question that each of us has been hurt by the words and actions of others, but unprocessed traumas can directly impact the outcome of our lives.

> "Words matter, how do you want to be remembered?"
> —Leslie Lowe

Just ask Nichole Mischke.

Nichole says she knew she was big for her size, but hearing her third grade class break out in laughter after a classmate said something cruel about her was enough to put her on a path that would practically kill her.

"Hey you guys! Nichole is eating a sandwich for a snack, that is why she is so fat!"

That was the day I started to believe the lie that my worth was defined by what my body looked like.

I felt so consumed and out of control. In my mind bulimia was probably going to kill me and there was nothing I could do about it.

Initially, I didn't think I had a problem, but before I knew it I was binging and purging sometimes more than a dozen times a day, every day, during my college years. I was secretly buying food on a credit card until I maxed it out at $5,000. I would go floor-to-floor in my five-story college dorm and raid all the kitchens, not caring that the food I was taking belonged to other broke college kids.

Ultimately it was the fear of death that woke me up from living my shallow existence.

My list of shameful behaviors to accommodate my eating disorder is embarrassingly long, but I share the shameful parts for two reasons: The first reason is that contrary to what you might think, freedom and healing in the most powerful forms come when you share your shame. The second reason is that I know my details will help someone else out there reading this know that they are not alone. You have to shed your shame. Shame tells us we're not good enough and unworthy. Shame makes us care too much what other people think. Shame is a liar and it's keeping you from fully embracing and loving all of you. Admitting my shame didn't isolate me like I was afraid it would, it actually brought me more community and deeper relationships into my life.

Decide today that instead of chasing something external to find your worth, you are going to turn inside yourself and start listening to that little voice that's been there ever since you were young. The voice that told you you could be anything you wanted to be in this world. The voice that longed to create something. The voice that sparks passion in your life.

I am eternally grateful that I woke up to that voice. I feel like I'm exactly where I'm supposed to be and I feel like I'm living my life in complete alignment with greater purpose.

We hope Leslie and Nichole's stories have empowered you to know that you do not have to live with the negative words of others, nor should you use those words when you are talking to yourself. We have the power to train our brains to think positively. Is it time to change your narrative?

Turning a Negative into a Positive

There is nothing more attractive than a positive person. A positive person radiates joy that makes others want to be around them. They leave others feeling energized because the conversation was enlightening. You rarely hear a positive person talk negatively about another because they have learned that talking about others does not make anyone feel good. Here are a few ways to turn the negative into a positive.

Begin by Standing Up for What You Believe In

There is strength in our voices, but only if we know how to use our words to lift others up, not to tear them down. Try speaking without haste and carelessness. Instead, be thoughtful with your words and use them to create a positive outcome.

Learn to Lead With Love

You can't live a positive life with a negative mind

© happydancing/Shutterstock.com

© ForGaby/Shutterstock.com

We all know that bad things happen in our world every day, but by being intentional—not just open-minded, but open-hearted—we can start to change the way our world looks and how we see others. Go out of your way to help others. Before long it will be a habit that makes you feel very good.

Practice Forgiveness

Forgiveness is a virtue not fit for the faint of heart. But learning how to exercise forgiveness frees you up to add more positivity in your life. Forgiveness is like setting down your emotional baggage that may not have been yours to carry in the first place. We urge you to read more on forgiveness and its healing powers if something or someone is weighing you down.

Forgive others but also learn how to forgive yourself. No human is perfect. We all make mistakes. Forgiveness allows us to move forward while still creating boundaries that others need to respect.

Hurt People, Hurt People

That's not a typo: Hurt people do hurt people. What that means is that, even if you do your best to be kind and considerate, you may still be judged negatively by others. This is not a reflection of your failings; rather, it is a reflection on where the others are coming from. People often behave in the only way they know how. Recognizing this can help you become a little more compassionate towards others, and thereby, lower your worry about what others think of you. ("How not to worry about what others think of you")

It is also important to recognize that we do not have to accept the harsh words of critical people. Difficult and judgmental people are not just hard on others, they are hard on themselves, too. More often than not, it is a past trauma that is still affecting them, but you do not have to accept their bad behavior. It is not your baggage to carry. By simply stating "That's not true," or saying "You should hear how nasty you sound," or asking, "What did you mean by that?" allows that person to think about his or her own words.

If the behavior continues and you are in a work or school setting, report it to human resources or the school counselor. Companies and schools are less tolerant toward bullies now than ever before because they can be held liable if they are aware of a situation. If you are in a bad relationship *please* get the help you need and deserve. Whatever you do, **do not lash out**.

When Is It okay Not to Care What Others Think About Us?

We are social creatures that spend much of our time looking and longing for connections. It is no wonder we care so much about what others think of us.

Answering the question "When is it okay not to care?" may be different for everyone. Some may say never. We should always care. Others will say I really do not care. Researchers would probably tell you the answer should lie somewhere in the middle. "Most of us are guilty of worrying too much about what others think of us. Studies show that we consistently overestimate how much, and how badly, others think about us and our failings. An unfortunate consequence of this is that we are far more inhibited and far less spontaneous and joyful than we could be." ("How not to worry about what others think of you")

It is self-destructive to constantly be caring about what others think of us.

© Brasil Creativo/Shutterstock.com

"Constantly wondering whether others like us enough can evoke anxiety, leading to neediness and insecurity, which in turn drive others away from us. This can propel a vicious cycle, resulting ultimately in loss of self-respect and social alienation." ("How not to worry about what others think of you")

When you know in your heart of hearts that your intentions are good, or that you have paid a penance for a past offense, that is a good sign that it is time to move forward and stop focusing on the negative.

Surround yourself with people who build you up, not tear you down.

Self-Esteem

Self-image and self-esteem are often used interchangeably, but they are different.

Brian Tracy, author of *The Psychology of Achievement*, says, "The best definition of self-esteem is, 'how much you like yourself.'" (Tracy, 1994)

Self-esteem is a belief. Your self-esteem is how you *feel* about the image you have of yourself and how you judge your worth. Your words are powerful. Be careful how you use them.

"Part of developing healthy self-esteem is making a commitment to yourself not to try to please the world," according to an article in Psychology Today. ("Eight traits of people with healthy self-esteem")

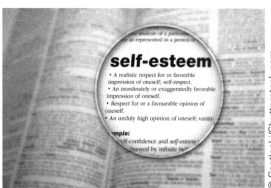

© Castleski/Shutterstock.com

What Is Holding Us Back?

Why is it that we sometimes do not achieve what we are hoping for? Is something holding us back? Quite possibly it is our self-image and/or self-esteem. If we do not feel that we are deserving of success or not good enough, we hold ourselves back—we do not take the risk or we proceed cautiously. There are many ways that we decrease our chances of success because of the way we view ourselves deep down inside.

We have seen numerous people in our lifetime who have been passed over for a position, demoted, or lost their jobs because of poor self-image and self-esteem. We believe working on, and developing, a healthy self-image and self-esteem by forming good self-compassion will open doors you never imagined possible. We have also witnessed the most amazing leaders create healthy environments for people to achieve success because they valued not only themselves, but also those around them.

Positive Reinforcement Goes a Long Way

How did you know you were good at certain subjects in school and not so good at others? When did you start to think about what you might want to do/be when you grow up? I (one of your authors) recall two very different experiences growing up that helped skew my view of myself. When I was in second grade, back in the days when you received letter grades on your report card, I got A's on every subject except Art and Science. I got C's in both those subjects. To this day I can picture that report card and remember how I dreaded any art project and then I developed

© Marie Maerz/Shutterstock.com

what I remember my mom calling a "mental block" about science. In other words, those grades created a self-fulfilling prophecy for me. To me, a "C" meant I was really bad at something. (I have to laugh a bit now, because as a college professor I tell my students often that in reality, "C" should mean average!) Luckily for me, I had parents who worked very hard to help me shift my perceptions about my abilities in Art and Science.

When I started third grade my parents put a huge, floor to ceiling bulletin board that was about 3 or 4 feet wide on the wall in my bedroom. Any time I brought home the artwork I did at school my parents proudly displayed it on the bulletin board. That board was packed solid in no time. The message I received was that my work *was valued* and that I should be proud of what I have done. Now, I am no Picasso today, but I do feel better about my creative talents.

> "Outstanding leaders go out of their way to boost the self-esteem of their personnel. If people believe in themselves, it's amazing what they can accomplish."
> —Sam Walton

Similarly, my parents cheered me on and supported my efforts when I competed in the Science Fair in fourth grade. I remember them clipping the weather report from the daily newspaper for me to put on my poster board as I tracked weather patterns for a month. I cannot remember if I got first, second, or third place, but I do remember that I got a ribbon and it wasn't just for participation! What matters most was my parents' support and encouragement, once again, which helped me to realize that my abilities *were* valued after all.

Developing a Healthy Self-Esteem

Anything worthwhile requires work. We cannot think of any better investment than to put the work into yourself. The payoff will be huge.

Here are some techniques others have used to strengthen their self-esteem:

1. **"Practice reflection.** Take 5 to 10 minutes daily to sit quietly and dwell on your positive traits, for example, intelligence, ability to get along with others, and athletic skills. Focus on your successes in the areas you've decided to think about. Recall that you were able to succeed, despite some initial fears. Apply that same kind of thinking to any upcoming event you find challenging. Tell yourself you plan to face any difficulties and overcome them.

2. **Try vivid imagery.** Use your imagination to see a scene before it occurs. Such a scene might include a conversation with a difficult coworker, a talk with a good friend who is going through a rough time, or a dreaded encounter with a parent. Imagine the scene vividly and rehearse what you plan to say. Anticipate the very worst that could happen, and imagine how you would deal with the worst-case scenario. Then imagine how you want the scene to turn out.

3. **Apply constructive self-talk.** Words shape your perceptions and thinking. Examine your use of words in reference to yourself. If you wrote down five adjectives to describe yourself how many would be positive and how many negative? It would be unrealistic to use nothing but positive language in describing yourself, but do try to make the ratio four to one in favor of positive over negative. For example, as you anticipate a difficult conversation with someone, tell yourself, 'I'm calm, prepared, poised, smart, and a little nervous.'

4. **Keep a sense of humor about yourself.** If you take yourself too seriously, you're bound to find it hard to live up to your expectations. Humor has the double advantage of relieving tension and raising self-esteem. One psychiatrist has a card taped to his bathroom mirror that reads, *'This person is not to be taken seriously.'* Good advice.

5. **Use your critical thinking skills** to measure whether your image of yourself is really accurate or is simply a projection by others of how you should look and act. Remember Eleanor Roosevelt's words: "No one can make you feel inferior without your consent."

6. **Attack self-destructive beliefs.** Psychotherapist Albert Ellis (1988, Ellis & Harper, 1973) and other cognitive therapists would argue that you could accomplish this by understanding why these beliefs are unrealistic and substituting more realistic ones. Engage in self-affirmation. Remind yourself of your successes (Aronson, Cohen, & Nail, 1998; Aronson, Wilson, & Akert, 1999).

7. **Avoid comparing yourself to others.** Social media makes it easy to constantly compare ourselves with others. We might often feel like the grass is always greener on the other side of the fence. "Social Comparison theory states that we compare ourselves to others so that we can get a feel for how our talents and abilities measure up." (K-H 3rd Edition, Communicating Effectively). The last thing you want to be is your own harshest critic, but oftentimes we are. If there's something you want to change about yourself make it a priority to write down steps in which to get there.

8. **Seek out and interact with people** who habitually build you up rather than tear you down. You can often choose who you want to be around.

9. **Work on projects that will result in success.** This does not mean that you never take chances, but you'll be happier completing tasks that turn out positively rather than poorly. We tend to enjoy those activities we do well." (Caputo, Hazel, McMahon, & Dannels, 2002, p. 93)

> **"Comparison is the thief of joy."**
> —Theodore Roosevelt

The Core of Me

© viphotos/Shutterstock.com

Have you ever stopped to reflect on your own values? What do you believe, deep down, about how you should live your life?

Your core values support your beliefs, and they are the motivation behind the actions you take. Surprisingly, very few of us stop to think about what our core values are and how they play out in our everyday lives. "America relies on the freedom that the U.S. Armed Forces provides and expects that it can trust the Department of Defense to act in a manner that is ethical, moral and with integrity," says Colonel Scot Heathman, Vice Commander, 92nd Air Refueling Wing, Fairchild Air Force Base who knows the importance of developing core values in the men and women who serve our country.

U.S. Air Force core values: Integrity First, Service Before Self and Excellence in All We Do. This is the foundation that sets the condition for our culture, how we execute our missions and how we preserve our profession. When we fail to live up to our core values, our culture begins to erode. The very fabric of our service, if not restored, will eventually start to negatively sway the public perception of the military.

If someone were to ask you what your core values are, would you be able to answer quickly or would you ask for a little time to think about it? There are numerous self-assessment tools available that help you define what your core values are. If you have never taken the time to reflect on your values, we highly recommend that you do. (Exercise at the end of the chapter).

If you live your life consistently by holding true to your values, the more likely you are to have high self-esteem. People who uphold their beliefs and values tend to like and respect themselves more. Know what is important to you and abide by your deepest values in all that you do and say. Here is an example of a values statement written by one of the author's children as a requirement in a course he took in college:

> *I strive to incorporate God in all aspects of my life. I strive to be competent in everything I put my mind to. I remain ambitious towards my goals without compromising my integrity. I attempt to be honest with myself and with others in order to stay true to my other values. I incorporate respect into every action, because if I do not treat others with respect, how can I ask for it in return? I strive to remain empathetic towards others, as I do not know their whole stories. I strive to remain dedicated through the struggles of life, without losing my passion and vigor for my goals and life.—Colin (age 18)*

Now 27, Colin still believes his core values have helped him succeed in life. He is now enjoying a job as a golf professional with an admired reputation in his community.

(Photo taken by Colleen McMahon.)

There are times in our lives when our beliefs and values are compromised or even challenged. Ask yourself how you will feel when you let yourself down when your actions do not line up with who you say you are. We have all had this happen. Do not beat yourself up, but learn from the experience and resolve to return to your core values and beliefs.

In addition to abiding by your beliefs and values, think about how you talk to yourself. Yes, we do talk to ourselves; all the time, as a matter of fact. Remember at the beginning of the chapter when we asked you what you see when you look in the mirror? Your typical response will reflect your self-image. How you talk to yourself (positively or negatively) is an extension of your self-esteem. If you speak positively

Source: Colleen McMahon

to yourself, "I've got this!" "I am strong," "I feel great!" "I like myself," you are more likely to be a happy, successful person.

Conversely, if you constantly give yourself messages of inadequacy or you are always telling yourself that you are less than, or not as smart, handsome, or pretty as others, you are more likely to suffer from low self-esteem and social anxiety. It is quite challenging, if not impossible, to be successful if you constantly engage in negative self-talk.

How easy is it for you to accept a compliment? Are you the kind of person who downplays the compliment or disagrees with the person giving you the compliment? If someone tells you he or she likes what you are wearing, do you respond with, "Oh, this old thing? I couldn't find anything else to wear today," or do you graciously say "Thank you"? The response you give directly reflects whether or not you have high or low self-esteem. Accepting a compliment politely does not mean you are cocky or full of yourself. You are simply acknowledging the kind words from another person, and in turn, making the other person feel good.

Most of us, we hope, want to be liked, to be accepted, and to be successful. Setting positive expectations for yourself is another technique you can use to ensure positive outcomes in your life. You *do have* control over your expectations. In the article, Developing self-esteem is key to your success, Karen Chaston emphasizes: "Believing you can do it. Believing you deserve it. Believing you will get it." (Chaston, 2018) Why not expect positive outcomes and watch them come to life? Expect to do wonderful things and achieve your goals. It is likely that you will!

© bluelela/Shutterstock.com

"Generally, people who like themselves tend to like others and feel confident around them. Those who do not care much for themselves, often do not like others either. People generally feel most loving toward others when they feel good about themselves." (Caputo et al., 2002, p. 91)

> "A strong, positive self-image is the best possible preparation for success."
> —Dr. Joyce Brothers

It may make you uneasy, but asking yourself the tough questions about who you are, where you come from, and how these events have shaped your life brings you one step closer to creating your own positive narrative. You should be the true authors of your life's story because what you think and how you view yourself is really what matters most.

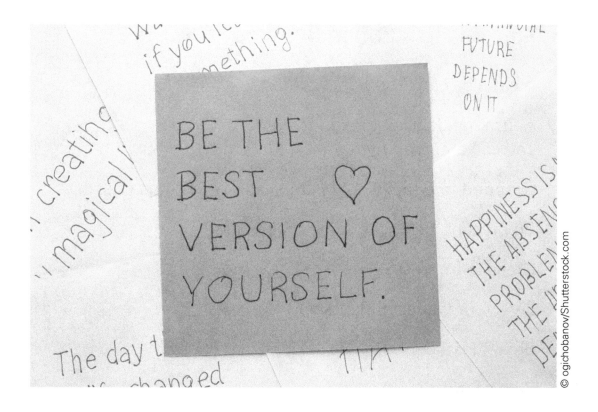

© ogichobanov/Shutterstock.com

Bottom line: We all deserve to be the best version of ourselves. The more we know ourselves, the more confident we become. It is easier to accept others when we accept ourselves. Learn from the past, embrace the present, and look forward to what is yet to come, knowing that you are creating a ***Reputation by Design*** that will open doors to an exciting future!

Image and Reputation Builders

* A simple Thank You!

* A firm handshake, look in the eye,
  and call a person by name.

* Respond to e-mails, texts, and calls as soon as possible.

* Be present, be engaged, and be willing.

* Dress to Impress

* Live your values and ethics.

* Be a model citizen.

* Be grateful.

Try this:

Take some time to try the following exercise. Begin by picking out some difficult but achievable challenge you face next week. Such a challenge could include a tough exam, a meeting with a difficult person, or a presentation you need to give. Then for ten minutes, do the following: Start by focusing on your strengths ('I am bright, confident, good with people, and so on'). Spend about 4 minutes concentrating on these strengths. Don't let any negative thoughts intrude. Now imagine the challenging situation in advance. See the place and/or the people involved. Rehearse how you're going to deal with the difficulties that will probably occur. Imagine the worst that could happen. How would you deal with the worst? Now imagine the best that could happen. How will you deal with that possibility? Now see yourself in control. Finally, repeat to yourself some positive phrases such as 'I'm confident, in control, and able to handle this situation.'" (Caputo et al., 2002, p. 97)

Do this:

I'm Good at Something:

Talk to between seven and ten people who you think know you well (family members, friends, significant others, a boss) and ask them to tell you something that they think you are good at. Brainstorm for yourself, too, the things that come to mind that you think you are good at (sometimes this is harder for us to do).

Pick one of those things, and come up with a 1 to 2 minute story that illustrates something that you are good at. Why? Often when we are in a job interview we are asked about our strengths. If you can tell a story that illustrates one of your strengths, it is more likely that the listener will remember what you talked about. For example, if you determine that you are good at *problem solving*, tell a story about a time that you worked through a situation and came up with a clever solution to a sticky situation.

Write the story in the space below.

Explore your values:

When we think of our values, we are focusing on what our priorities are and what makes us truly happy. They are the things that you feel are important for the way you live your life, personally and professionally. You can measure your success if you are matching your values with your behaviors. Your values are relatively stable, but they can shift at different phases of your life. For example, your values as a student might shift when you get a job, get married, or have children.

In the space below, brainstorm a list of 20 words that come to mind when you think of your values. Do not think too hard about this. Just write whatever comes to mind.

1.   6.   11.   16.
2.   7.   12.   17.
3.   8.   13.   18.
4.   9.   14.   19.
5.   10.   15.   20.

Now, in the next section prioritize your top values. See if you can zero in on your top 5 to 7.

1.

2.

3.

4.

5.

6.

7.

Once you have narrowed it down, in the space below create your own values statement.

_____

_____

_____

_____

_____

_____

_____

References

Caputo, J. S., Hazel, H. C., McMahon, C. A., & Dannels, D. (2002). *Communicating effectively: Linking thought and expression.* Dubuque, IA: Kendall/Hunt Pub.

Chaston, K. (2018, January 29). *Developing self-esteem is key to your success.* Retrieved March 31, 2019 from https://www.thebusinesswomanmedia.com/developing-self-esteem-key-success

Eight traits of people with healthy self-esteem. (n.d.). Retrieved March 31, 2019 from https://www.psychologytoday.com/us/blog/hope-relationships/201608/eight-traits-people-healthy-self-esteem

Hazel, H. (1987). *The art of talking to yourself and others.* Kansas City, MO: Sheed & Ward.

How not to worry about what others think of you. (n.d.). Retrieved from https://www.psychologytoday.com/us/blog/sapient-nature/201603/how-not-worry-about-what-others-think-you

Our brain's negative bias. (n.d.). Retrieved March 31, 2019 from https://www.psychologytoday.com/us/articles/200306/our-brains-negative-bias

The negativity bias: Why the bad stuff sticks and how to overcome it. (n.d.). Retrieved March 31, 2019 from https://www.psycom.net/negativity-bias

Tracy, B. (1994). *The psychology of achievement.* Boston, MA: Simon & Schuster Audiobooks.

Warrell, M. (2017, October 2). *Is negativity bias sabotaging your success?* Retrieved from https://www.forbes.com/sites/margiewarrell/2017/09/30/combat-negativity-bias

chapter 4

YOU ARE WHAT YOU TWEET

© solomon7/Shutterstock.com

The fastest way to lose your credibility is to post things that offend people.

People who are active on social media post what is important to them and on their minds at the moment. Your passions show up in pictures, posts, snaps, and tweets. Mason loves skiing. Emma loves fashion. Olivia is a foodie. Noah loves to drink. Sophia loves herself #alot!

> "The outcome is always in your control, choose wisely on what you post and it will pay off in the end."
> —John

"If someone has an entire library of selfies on their social media, that is never a good sign," says John, an HR Advisor/Recruiter who actively recruits college graduates. He uses social media as a tool to get to know more about a potential employee.

John offers this advice. "Social media can be used as an opportunity for a first impression. If you want to communicate that you are a party animal, post pictures of you shot gunning a beer. If you want to communicate that you care about your community, post pictures of you and your friends volunteering."

Just about anyone (your colleagues, potential employers, boss, and anyone else) can see exactly what you are posting on social media. That is why it is *so* important to be deliberate and thoughtful about what you share and the image you are portraying. Furthermore, make sure that you periodically conduct an online search of yourself to see what is showing up. If there is anything even remotely harmful to your reputation, immediately take steps to get it removed.

© Puchongart/Shutterstock.com

Social Media Is a Big, Glaring Spotlight on YOU!

The pictures you post leave an impression on people that allow them to form an opinion of you.

The opinion that could open doors for better opportunities or close them without you ever knowing they were interested in the first place. "If I see a lot of alcohol on their page, the conversation usually stops there," says Sarah, an HR Recruiter for a utilities company.

The posts we share are a reflection of our values, thoughts, and feelings. "Before you post, ask yourself this question, "If this picture were to land in the lap of a person who wanted to destroy my chances of capturing my dream job . . . would I still post it?" Sounds harsh, but it has happened, and it will continue to happen as long as social media is around. Social media gives people more ammunition *than ever before* to expose our missteps, mistakes, and misunderstandings.

What most people do not realize is that you represent more than just yourself. Your employer wants to see you as an asset, not a liability. "Don't give your future employer an opportunity to pass you up. It's not worth the 100 likes," says Nick Aaro, a recent Arizona State University graduate. A company will spend money training you to hone and sharpen your skills. They will compensate you for your time and expertise. Recruiting is big business and that is why finding the perfect candidate is important. They want to make sure they are putting their money and time into a person who will grow into a leader, climb the career ladder, and give them a maximum return on their investment.

Golden Rule

If your job or your boss makes you miserable, don't post about it. It's a great way to lose your paycheck. It is so much easier to get a job when you have one because you don't come across as desperate. Plus, you will need references in the future. Play it safe! No matter how upset you are, don't rant.

People say things on social media that they would never say in person. Do not get caught up in drama or post just to get attention. Remember: humor rarely translates as "funny," especially since messages have very little context. Just ask Justine Sacco. This is one of the headlines about her from the New York Times:

"How One Stupid Tweet Blew Up Justine Sacco's Life"
New York Times, Jon Ronson February 2015

Justine Sacco earned a very large paycheck as a public relations executive with one of the most successful online firms in New York.

She learned the hard way that humor doesn't translate.

Sacco thought she was being funny when she carelessly posted on her Twitter page . . . "Going to Africa. Hope I don't get AIDS. Just kidding. I'm white!"

While she was in flight to South Africa her tweet went viral, and the online world was in an uproar over it. Comments like, "Oh man, @JustineSacco is going to have the most painful phone-turning-on moment ever when her plane lands" and "We are about to watch this @Justine Sacco (expletive) b——get fired in REAL time. Before she even knows she's getting fired." Those were a couple tame tweets being fired off as Sacco was inflight, completely unaware of what was happening online.

So how can a person with less than 200 Twitter followers quickly become the #1 worldwide Twitter trend? Easy! All you need is one person with many followers to share and the mass online destruction will move at the speed of light.

This tweet infuriated thousands who perceived Sacco as racist with a white privilege attitude. She claims it was a joke and figured no one in this day and age would take her words literally. It especially wasn't funny to her family who lived in South Africa and are longtime activists for racial equality.

When her plane landed in South Africa, her world as she knew it, was about to fall apart. Sacco not only lost her job and six figure salary, she also lost her reputation, and her company, IAC, risked losing theirs as well.

Sacco became the subject of public shaming on a worldwide scale. The hashtag #hasJustinelandedyet had people glued to their phones to see if anyone would snap a picture of her at the airport when she arrived in South Africa. Guess what? Someone did. Her picture was posted for the entire world to see.

We will talk about repairing your reputation in the following chapters, but what we know for sure is that it took Sacco years to recover from the mistake that she had made. Since then, there have been countless others just like her who wound up in the unemployment line because of an error in judgment they could have prevented.

These are just a few cautionary tales that serve as a reminder to think about the potential consequences before you post. This tweet by a former major league baseball player, now radio personality Mike Bacsik **"congrats to all the dirty mexicans in San Antonio."** (Barri-Segal, 2018) went viral after the San Antonio Spurs beat the Dallas Mavericks. These careless words ultimately cost him his job. While he did apologize for his racist comment, it was just another reminder that we need to think before we tweet.

A teacher was forced to resign from her teaching job because she posted a picture just like this on her Facebook page. Now she is fighting to get her job back.

© Roman Samborskyi/Shutterstock.com

"Different Jobs have Different Levels of Background Checks."

© Nestor Rizhniak/Shutterstock.com

News Director, Kelly Hatmaker has spent the last 20 years focusing on computer assisted reporting and data driven journalism. "People who are looking to become teachers for example might find their social media under a much stronger microscope because they are expected to be responsible for minors."

Many people think they are safe because their social media accounts are private. They are not. "There are some very smart people who spend their days trying to figure out ways around our on-line security restrictions—including the locks you put on social media accounts." Hatmaker goes on to say, "Remember, that you have control over what you post, so make sure that what you share shines the most positive light on you."

Social Media Can Be Fun!

Twin BOYS coming this summer!
#howardfamilyof5 #twinbabyboy... See More

178   56 Comments

♡ Love   💬 Comment

There are many bright sides to social media. The invention of many apps has helped create movements, raise money for worthy causes, launched businesses, helped people find love, and keeps family members connected to one another. It has helped spread kindness. We also cannot overlook the social support it provides. You post your good news, you get a bunch of "likes" and you feel supported. In turn, you feel better about yourself. You post your sad news, say a death in your family, and you get empathy, prayers, and words of wisdom and hope sent your way. According to a recent study done by The Pew Research Center, many teens agree "that social media make them more connected, allow them to interact with a diverse group of people and make them feel like they have someone who would support them in a tough time." (Anderson, Jiang, Anderson, & Jiang, 2018)

Many People Have Secured Jobs Using Social Media

LinkedIn reports that roughly 20,000 U.S. companies use their site to recruit new talent. It is a place that connects you to business professionals. You can also follow companies you are interested in learning more about. Think of it as your online resume. Do not forget to make sure your LinkedIn picture is the one you like the most. That first impression, even online, goes a long way!

Like ME!!

It feels good to be Liked!

> *"Likes are always an indicator of social standing, at my age," says an anonymous 17-year-old survey respondent. "As someone who gets anxious and occasionally struggles with self-esteem, the amount of Likes on my posts can be both hugely uplifting or depressing."* ("Both hugely uplifting and depressing")

It is the moment that we post something that keeps us coming back for more. "The same brain circuits that are activated by eating chocolate and winning money are activated when teenagers see large numbers of 'likes' on their own photos or the photos of peers in a social network, according to findings from a new study in which researchers scanned teens' brains while they used social media." ("Social media 'likes' impact teens' brains and behavior")

We get a sense that our online reputation has been enhanced when people respond favorably to our tweets or posts. And the dopamine reward we get gives us a physiological "high." When something makes us feel that good, it is likely that we will want to repeat it. That is human nature. Some research actually suggests that our addiction to dopamine is stronger than that of caffeine or alcohol.

"Kids aren't the only one addicted to their phones."

Social media can be a bad habit, even an addiction, for many people, especially the youth. When we are young we really desire to fit into social circles. We will do things that go against our gut just to be liked. Putting a phone in a child's hands gives them nonstop access to many social media sites when their brains are not prepared for such a barrage of information. This can carry some pretty heavy consequences. Research shows our brains are not fully developed until we reach our mid-20s.

"The last areas to mature are the frontal areas. The ones we use for executive functions like planning, inhibition, reasoning,

"We don't have a choice on whether we DO social media, the question is how well we DO it."
—Erik Qualman

© OmniArt/ Shutterstock. com

i am so thankful i had a childhood before technology took over

© AnnaElizabeth photography/Shutterstock.com

and problem solving. It's like everything is ready, except the part that is supposed to keep it all in check, which is why we see such *interesting* behavior in teenagers." (Quora, 2017)

Many parents think it is an invasion of privacy to monitor their child's online behavior, but it is not. We believe it is a parent's responsibility. They are minors. They are not fully capable of rationalizing what may happen if they post without thinking of the consequences. By not having the capacity to fully understand the consequences of posting pictures, making comments or remarks on social media sites that have the shelf life of FOREVER, teens or young adults can find themselves in serious trouble. It is our job to protect them from cyberbullying, or allowing them to engage in behavior that may shape their image or reputation in a harmful way. We have come to learn that social media is flooded with rumors and bullying. While many adults can make the statement "I am so thankful I had a childhood before technology took over," our children cannot say the same. Their world is so different and that is why we need to help them navigate their way through it.

Mila's Milestone

Mila was a heavy social media user in high school, running two social media sites for clubs at school, in addition to her own, it started to become too overwhelming. "I was constantly seeing socials all the time and as an insecure high school student, it started to get to me, the constant parading of other people's 'oh-so-perfect' lives that they would present online," bothered Mila, she says.

"When I started crying and freaking out over my follower- to -following ratio on Instagram, I decided it was time to take a break from social media."

Mila told us she began a one-month "social media cleanse" from all follower responsive sites like (Instagram, Twitter, Facebook, Snapchat, Pinterest), "anything where I constantly had other people's lives shoved in my face."

One month quickly turned into 8 months for Mila. "It began to feel really good taking a break from everyone else. When you're with people all day at school and then figuratively with them all day at home, it gets exhausting to be "on" all the time. It felt good not having to compare myself to other people's angles and falsified photos where they Facetune their noses to the point that they don't even look like themselves."

__Now a junior in college she looks at social media like this . . .". I use social media mainly for work purposes now—I try to stay off of social media if I know it'll make me feel upset. Sometimes I have to take a break from these platforms to evaluate why I care so much about other people's lives. I do spend a lot of time on Twitter though, just to stay relevant with the news".

What do *you* think are some of the reasons that social media is making people feel bad? Two things stand out, in particular. The first is social comparison. We see other people doing great things (or so they *say so* online) or enjoying great vacations or experiences. One person's happiness is another person's jealousy. When we see how everyone else is living this great life, and ours does not compare, we may think that our life pretty much stinks.

> "Social Media is training us to compare our lives, instead of appreciating everything we are. No wonder why everyone is always depressed."
> —Bill Murray

The second very common reason social media makes people feel badly is what is known as FOMO, or fear of missing out. Again, we go online, see other people at social functions, parties, showing up in group selfies, and we may feel

badly because we are not enjoying all the perceived "fun" activities that our peers are boasting about online.

Camden's Connection

Camden, a junior at the University of Washington, felt he was wasting too much time checking his sites. He aspires to be a doctor and didn't need the distractions.

"I believe that this enlightenment of 'going off the grid' has allowed me to open my eyes more in society and recognize the trend we are nearing, and ultimately one I would like to fix."

Instead of feeling more connected to people he felt the opposite.

"In many ways it has actually isolated the public from one another."

While he still checks sites like Reddit, his absence has been a breath of fresh air.

"My 'being-out-of-the-loopness' has allowed me to focus my passions rather than being distracted by certain gossipy information within social groups."

We know that social media can be both a blessing and a curse. Maintaining a trustworthy personal online presence should be a priority for all of us. As Vincent Filak, author of *Dynamics of Media Writing* emphasizes, ". . . the more trust people place in you, the better off you will be, so put effort into this at every turn."

It is also why your online reputation should align with your values, character, morals, and integrity, and if for one second you question whether or not you should post something that may be misconstrued, misunderstood, or mistaken . . . Don't!! Doing social media right can enhance your reputation, make you a valuable asset to your workplace, bring you customers, and lifelong relationships. Be intentional with your words. We have all been told to think before you speak. Think before you Tweet.

Lonely and Depressed? You Are Not Alone

That is why you should know your ABCDs for yourself and for the ones you love, because studies have linked online use to these issues facing our country. Another reason to monitor yours and their activities is because studies have shown that social media can be detrimental to mental health. Many negative effects of an excessive or obsessive online presence include:

Anxiety

Adolescents and teens are experiencing anxiety more now than ever before. There are so many uncertainties and fears. Some have to do with things that they cannot even control. They may experience anxiety because they are not getting enough "likes" on something they posted, or simply be anxious because they cannot spend as much time surfing through their social media platforms as they would like. Spending too much time worrying about who said what about whom, or who did or did not react to what they posted, can also cause them to lose sleep.

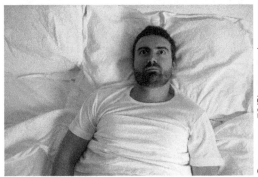

© tommaso79/Shutterstock.com

Bad Sleeping Habits

Yes, social media can make you lose sleep.

Melatonin is the hormone in your body that regulates sleep. High levels of melatonin can help you sleep while low levels can keep you awake. Harvard Health Publishing of Harvard Medical School says that any kind of light can reduce how much melatonin your body makes (which is why some people love wearing sleep masks or having blackout curtains). However, blue light, which is emitted from the screens of your smartphone and iPads, lessen your melatonin levels even more. That said, social media scrolling, especially at night, could really put your circadian rhythm out of tune. "Getting a good night's sleep is also crucial for helping our brain to be working at its best," says Dr. Craig Lammers, PhD, a psychologist who regularly sees patients who deal with these issues.

Communication Issues

"Nonverbal communication is gradually becoming one of the dominant forms of interpersonal interaction, negatively affecting people's ability to deal with personal contact and meet the reactions and emotions of other people in real life." ("The effects of social media on communication skills: Cause and effect essay samples")

Studies are showing that interpersonal communication is suffering as a result of heavy social media use. "One of the big problems in modern interpersonal communication is the lack of interest people have for face-to-face communication; even today, there are many people (especially millennials, or younger) who prefer to solve work or personal problems via social messaging systems." ("The effects of social media on communication skills: Cause and effect essay samples")

Communicating through social media can alienate a lot of people. The younger generation prefers to text while their parents and grandparents would much rather receive a phone call. This can alienate families from one another if they do not talk about these issues.

Facebook's corporate vision statement today says that people use it ". . . to stay connected with friends and family, discover what's going on in the world and share and express what matters to them." (Smithson, 2019) While this may be true, can you think of a family member or friend who no longer speak to each other because of an argument, disagreement, or comment that was started using social media? We can. Many of us have witnessed our own family and friends post outrageous statements that shock the ones they love.

Leaders understand that there are many ways in which to communicate. They try to be good at a lot of them while understanding a time and place for each one.

Depression

Recently, I had dinner with a friend, who is a child and adolescent psychologist, and I asked him if he dealt with any clients who had mental health issues resulting from social media use. He immediately gave it a clinical name: Facebook depression. Sure enough, I started researching, and "Facebook depression" is a term that correlates social media use among adolescents, tweens, and teens with depression.

Dr.Craig Lammers, Clinical Psychologist, says, "At its heart, 'Facebook Depression' is a concern resulting from our use of social media. Particularly for children and adolescents, a report by the American Academy of Pediatrics defines it as a type of depression that develops when someone spends time on social media sites and then begins to exhibit symptoms of depression due to the intensity of the online world. In my experience, I find this to be the result of people of any age who frequently compare themselves and their lives to the lives of people they are following on social media. Too often they see their lives as falling short or being 'less than' the people they are following. They have difficulty understanding that what they're seeing on social media may not be a full representation of what is happening in the other person's world, as usually people are only posting their successes, their travels and their accomplishments. In comparison, we may feel depressed, left out, or like we are failing. This can be particularly true during adolescence, when being like your peers is crucial in trying to develop your identity."

According to an article on Marketwatch.com, "Spending too much time on 'social media' sites like Facebook is making people more than just miserable. It may also be making them depressed." (Arends, 2019) The University of Pittsburgh Schools of the Health Sciences reports, "People who report using seven to 11 social media platforms had more than three times the risk of depression and anxiety than their peers who use zero platforms, even after adjusting for the total time spent on social media overall." (Arends, 2019) Furthermore, psychologists at the University of Pennsylvania discovered that "rates of depression and loneliness" decreased when people limited their social media use. (Arends, 2019)

Dr. Lammers suggests that we simply turn off our phones for short periods throughout each day. He says that, "None of us should be using our cell phone as an alarm clock, as this potentially introduces us to social media first thing in the morning." Finally, he notes that we need to seek a balance in our lives. We need to accept the fact that ". . . social media WILL be a part of 'our lives,' 'but should not be the primary or sole focus'."

Bottom line: We have created a bad habit of mindlessly scrolling, posting, and replying on social media. We need to be much more mindful if we want to develop an online presence that is positive and respectful. It is not only good for our state of mind; it is great for our reputation! Remember, we are creating our ***Reputation by Design***.

Reputation Builders	Reputation Destroyers
* Stay Positive	* Being Negative
* Engage With Other Users	* Placing Blame
* Make Sure Your Pictures Align With Your Values	* Not Responding To Questions
* Be Respectful	* Don't Be Rude
* Take a Break Once in Awhile	* Pictures With Lots of Alcohol
	* Check Your Ego at the Keyboard

Try this:

Take a walk in a public space without your phone. Count the amount of people on their phone versus direct conversation in a 10–15 minute period.
It will actually shock you! - Camden Bendickson

Do this:

My Social Media posts: to "Like" or not to "Like"

Look through your social media posts from the last month or so. Take notice of your top three posts that received the most "Likes" and/or positive comments. Next, take notice of the three posts that received little or no responses.

In pairs or small groups, discuss the similarities and differences among the kinds of posts that received the most "likes" and positive comments. How did the positive responses make you feel? Were there more similarities than differences when discussing with your partner/group? In the same pair or group, talk about how you felt when your bottom three posts received little or no responses. Why do you think the lack of response made you feel the way you did? What are some of the feelings you shared in common with your partner or group?

Finally, talk with your partner/group about what you *learned about yourself* and others after having completed this exercise.

Talk this over:

In a small group or with a partner, discuss whether or not you agree with the Bill Murray quote that was included in this chapter:

"Social Media is training us to compare our lives, instead of appreciating everything we are. No wonder why everyone is always depressed."
—Bill Murray

References

Anderson, M., Jiang, J., Anderson, M., & Jiang, J. (2018, November 30). Teens, Social Media & Technology 2018. Retrieved from https://www.pewinternet.org/2018/05/31/teens-social-media-technology-2018/

Arends, B. (2019, January 12). *More research says facebook can cause depression, this time among millennials.* Retrieved from https://www.marketwatch.com/story/new-study-claims-facebook-instagram-and-snapchat-are-linked-to-depression-2018-11-09

Barri-Segal. (2018, February 25). *The best social media posts that cost people their jobs.* Retrieved from https://www.cheatsheet.com/money-career/the-best-social-media-posts-that-cost-people-their-jobs.html

"Both hugely uplifting and depressing": How do social media likes affect you? (n.d.). Retrieved from http://www.newstatesman.com/science-tech/social-media/2017/01/both-hugely-uplifting-and-depressing-how-do-social-media-likes

Filak, V. F. (2019). *Dynamics of media writing adapt and connect.* Washington, DC: CQ Press, a division of Sage.

Harvard Health Publishing. (n.d.). *Blue light has a dark side.* Retrieved from http://www.health.harvard.edu/staying-healthy/blue-light-has-a-dark-side

Ronson, J. (2015, February 12). *How one stupid tweet blew up justine sacco's life.* Retrieved from https://www.nytimes.com/2015/02/15/magazine/how-one-stupid-tweet-ruined-justine-saccos-life.html

Quora. (2017, August 31). *Are teenagers' brains fully developed? Not when it comes to executive functions, says science.* Retrieved from https://www.forbes.com/sites/quora/2017/08/31/are-teenagers-brains-fully-developed-not-when-it-comes-to-executive-functions-says-science

Smithson, N. (2019, February 25). *Facebook Inc.'s mission statement & vision statement (an analysis).* Retrieved from http://panmore.com/facebook-inc-vision-statement-mission-statement

Social media "likes" impact teens' brains and behavior. (n.d.). Retrieved from https://www.psychologicalscience.org/news/releases/social-media-likes-impact-teens-brains-and-behavior.html

The effects of social media on communication skills: Cause and effect essay samples. (2017, October 2). Retrieved from https://academichelp.net/samples/academics/essays/cause-effect/the-effects-of-social-media.html

chapter 5

REPAIRING YOUR REPUTATION

Y ou have messed up! Failed miserably! Fallen from grace! Now what?

At one point in our lives, we have all made mistakes we are not proud of. We have embarrassed ourselves, beaten ourselves up over it, and have felt ashamed because of it, but at some point we need to start picking up the pieces and get back to living life, unless we like tripping over the same mess we cannot seem to clean up.

Just recently, Lori Laughlin, also known as Aunt Becky on the sitcom *Full House*, and her husband, fashion designer, Mossimo Giannulli were part of an alleged college admissions cheating scam to get their two daughters admitted into the University of Southern California.

© 3DProfi/Shutterstock.com

© Tinseltown/Shutterstock.com

The couple paid upwards of $500,000 to say that Olivia Jade and her sister were on the USC rowing team, which was not true. That bribery money is peanuts compared to the price of the shame and embarrassment the family is enduring.

The wholesome looking actress not only tarnished her squeaky-clean image, but also the reputation of her daughter Olivia Jade, a social media influencer with more than 1.4 million followers.

"She is definitely upset with her parents. This wasn't her idea," the source said of the influencer, who has been dropped by several beauty companies, including Sephora and TRESemmé, in the wake of the scandal. "She didn't care if she got into USC. She just wanted to focus on her business." ("Olivia Jade previously revealed her parents warned that...")

The ripple effect of lying, cheating, and getting caught will take an enormous toll on them both emotionally and financially. The value of the family's ruined reputation has been depleted. Not only was Olivia Jade fired from some of the companies she represented, her mother was also dropped from the *Hallmark* channel and will no longer appear on *Fuller House*. Both women run a huge risk of not getting chosen for future work because people tend to disassociate themselves from those with bad reputations. The assumption, right or wrong, is that you are part of the same group of friends or same family. Inevitably they will suffer from the same shaming.

> "It's ironic how fortune disappears once reputation and character is damaged."
> —Jon Michail

It does not matter where they go now or what they do, people will always see them in a different light. Laughlin will most likely be remembered for what she did, not for what she has done with her once successful career. It may be difficult for them to show their faces for a while because of how many people they have angered. "Olivia is hanging out with longtime friends, but that's it. She doesn't want to go out in public." ("Olivia Jade previously revealed her parents warned that…") The name calling on Olivia Jade's social media sites was relentless. To date, Olivia Jade has yet to post one thing on her Instagram page. We can only imagine how fearful she is to try.

To add insult to injury, prior to this scandal coming to light, Laughlin informed her daughter about the importance of having a good reputation. The headline in an article written by Joelle Goldstein of People magazine reads, "Olivia Jade previously revealed her parents warned that 'you only get one reputation.'"

We could write an entire book on people who have damaged their reputations in the past year alone. Caroline Knorr, of Common Sense Media (reported in The Spokesman-Review, Saturday, March 23, 2019) says, "From internet-famous celebs such as Logan Paul and PewDiePie, to pop culture influencers like Kylie Jenner, good role models can go bad." She goes on to say that, "Sometimes beloved celebrities, such as Michael Jackson, attract headlines in such a negative fashion that it's really hard to explain news coverage about them to kids who've looked up to them." ("When good role models go bad")

While the average time to repair your reputation is roughly four years, we do believe there is a right and wrong approach to trying, but it has to start with remorse. If you do not feel bad for what you did in the first place, you will never get yourself back on track. Repairing a damaged reputation requires a deliberate commitment to change.

The Comeback Kid

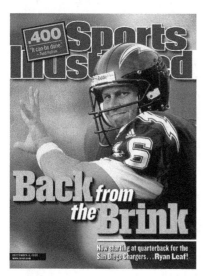

I had only heard the rumors about how arrogant Ryan Leaf was, but I had never met the guy personally. All I knew was that Ryan Leaf was one gifted athlete. Every single sportscaster covering his success as quarterback for Washington State University was in awe of his raw talent. But the word "cocky" was kicked around the newsroom when saying his name. I had even heard the **Big** joke about the **Big** man on campus.

"What's the difference between God and Ryan Leaf? God doesn't think he's Ryan Leaf."

Nonetheless, Ryan Leaf made it to The Big League in a big way. The San Diego Chargers selected him as the second overall pick in the 1998 NFL draft behind Peyton Manning. His four-year contract was worth $31.25 million, including a guaranteed signing bonus worth $11.25 million. It was the largest signing bonus ever paid to a rookie at that time.

While Manning's career led him to the Super Bowl several times and his success earned him most valuable player awards, Leaf's career was quite the opposite. Unfortunately, he "earned" the reputation as being, "The Biggest Bust in the NFL." Ultimately, Leaf bounced around the NFL for another 5 years before hanging up his jersey at the young age of 26. The years that followed included an addiction to painkillers, an attempt to take his life, time in prison, and ultimately a transformation that led to redemption.

Here is Leaf in his own words.

"When I came into the <u>NFL</u>, there were three things that were very important to me: money, power, and prestige. I was powerful now because I was a famous athlete. I had prestige because I was doing what everybody wanted to do. And I had a lot of money.

When I'm talking to parents, I tell them an analogy. My emotional level was kind of stunted when I was about 13, so I tell them to try this experiment at home: Give your 13-year-old child $31 million and see how that works out.

So I'm 21, have $31 million, and I wasn't responsible to anyone any more for money or really anything. If anybody said "no" to me, I would discard them from my life. That included my parents at one point. I just had zero perspective on what was important.

I spend a lot of time now working with young men coming into the NFL, or in college, and my biggest suggestion to them is, just because you're a good football player doesn't mean you're a good person. The ego that goes with being an athlete in this country is huge. We play a game.

But that game was important to me, and to millions of people across the country. I was always successful at that game, and I didn't fail until I got to the highest level, so a lot of my bad behavior was covered up by how I performed. Once my career started to go downhill, those behaviors were given a spotlight on a national level. I think it was my mother's worst fear that her son would be found out that way, on that stage. And I was.

I dealt with the media poorly. I dealt with my teammates poorly. I was now making $5 million a year and was miserable doing something I had wanted to do since I was 4. The third game of my career, we played Kansas City and I played as poorly as I've ever played in my life. I completed one of 15 passes and had two interceptions. I yelled at a reporter in a clip that's now famous, and I can almost narrow it down to a feeling where that was where my NFL career ended. Three games in, 22-year-old kid.

But I bounced around the league until 2002, from the Chargers to Tampa Bay to Dallas to Seattle. Everywhere I went, there was a little bit of a problem, this, that or the other. Until recently, I wasn't able to take accountability for that, and I didn't understand that throughout all that, I was the common denominator. I was the part that didn't't change.

You'll notice I'm saying nothing of drugs or alcohol, because they basically didn't exist for me. I didn't drink until my 18th birthday. I had never taken a drug in my life, other than Vicodin after surgeries, but I behaved the same way that addicts do every day. I was manipulative, narcissistic, deceitful, a thief.

When my career ended, I was only 28. I simply walked away from something I had wanted to do since I was 4 because I couldn't put up with it. I was tired of the criticism, tired of getting beat up physically and mentally on a daily basis. I just assumed everything would stay the same because I still had my three ideals: money, power, and prestige. So I just walked away from the game.

But now, my life came with a caveat. It came with the media and fans saying I was the biggest bust ever. My identity was wrapped up in not only being a football player but a failed football player, somebody who couldn't cut it. Not only that, I was a bad person.

One night, while I was in Las Vegas to see a fight, a gentleman offered me a couple of painkillers. Now remember, I'd taken them throughout my career because of surgeries, and they alleviated my physical pain every time. This would be the first time I took them for my emotional pain, and it worked. I always felt judged when I walked into a room. That night in Vegas, I'd walk into rooms and didn't feel judgment or fear. I felt numb, and I could just kind of be me—or who I thought was me. That went on for a long time.

Never knew a drug dealer. I could walk into a doctor's office and say, "Doc, give me some painkillers," and get them. I had been beaten up for a living as a quarterback. I always rationalized that those painkillers were something that were owed to me. I deserved them. I was doing the wrong thing the right way.

For a long time, I was able to feel numb from all the feelings I needed to feel. I tried to prove to everybody that everything was fine. If social media had existed back then, all that stuff you've seen from Johnny Manziel the past year—the private planes, the parties, the Cabo vacations—that would have been pretty identical to what my life looked like for the 2 years after I retired from football. Eventually, though, that money goes away.

It's hard to transition out of football. Even when you're super successful, guys who have played 18 or 20 years and have won four Super Bowls, they still have difficulty with that transition. They believe they're not ever going to do anything that important again. Well, I had it twofold. I thought I was super important because I was a football player, and I also felt I was a disappointment because I didn't live up to expectations and was considered a bust.

So I medicated and medicated. I started coaching young men and taking their pills from them, telling them I needed it. I wasn't a good criminal, and I got caught. I went to treatment and learned a different point of view. But being a drug addict, you learn how to manipulate people. I was good at it. I could say the right things, talk a good game, make people like me.

I guess it wasn't really vital that people like me, but it was essential that people knew me, knew how important I was. Sure enough, that backfires on you as well. You can't live a life where you're the center of all that. There has to be something much bigger.

I never thought I'd be someone sitting in a room and contemplating taking my life. I went into the bathroom, took a knife, and tried to slit my wrist. This was that 4-year-old boy who wanted to be a professional athlete. Now, I was 35, sitting in the bathroom, making the decision that it was better to be dead than alive.

How does that come about? Second pick in the draft. All these accolades that come with that. And it's gone.

It didn't work. I cut my wrist, but couldn't fully follow through with it. I was arrested the next day for going into the homes of friends and other people and taking their pills. Like I said, I never knew a drug dealer, so I had to find inventive ways to get what I needed. I wasn't a good criminal.

They threw me in a Montana jail cell on April 1, 2012. I would spend the next 32 months in prison. Nothing huge changed. My narcissism, my self-loathing existed pretty much through the whole period. I had a cellmate who was a combat veteran who had fought in Afghanistan and Iraq. He had done something terrible. He made a mistake that a lot of us have made ourselves. He drove drunk, and in his case, he happened to kill somebody that night.

About 26 months in, he got on me real hard one day about having my head buried in the sand. He said I didn't understand the value I had, not only to the guys in there but when I would get out. "Because Ryan," he told me, "You're going to get out at some point." So he told me that day that we were going to go down to the prison library and teach some other inmates how to read.

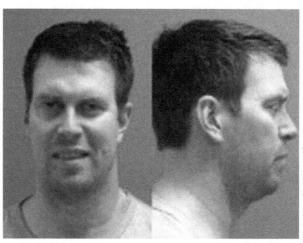

Handout/Handout/Getty

61

So I went. It was the first time in my life that I had ever been of service to anybody but myself. Ever. These men were vulnerable enough to ask for help at 40, 50, 60 years old, and they didn't know how to read. I started doing that and eventually a light came on for me. I don't know why it was something that simple, but it was. The self-loathing started to dissipate, and I knew that once I got out I had to make a 180-degree lifestyle change. I didn't know what it was going to look like, and I was going to need a lot of help from people I had probably hurt in my life.

Luckily for me, I had people in my life that unconditionally supported and loved me. When I walked out of that prison cell on Dec. 12, 2014, I was 32 months sober—for some reason, I chose not to use drugs in prison even though they were readily available—but it wasn't like I was cured. Just because I had removed the substance didn't mean those old behaviors didn't exist.

I knew I had to build a foundation. I went and sought treatment immediately when I got out. I was there for 90 days. Being in treatment when I was 3 years sober and living with people who were just detoxing was difficult. It taught me patience and a different perspective. I knew what was out there for me if I chose to continue my destructive behavior.

Most important, I knew being of service was going to be key. That's when I got hired as a driver for Transcend Recovery Community. Christian, their chief operating officer, told me, "Normally, we start people out at 10 bucks an hour, but we'll start you out at 15." I don't remember doing this, but he said I gave him the biggest bear hug you can imagine. To think I was making $5 million a year and was miserable, and then I was making $15 an hour and was super grateful for that. I'd never felt as valued as I did then.

That job ultimately became what I'm doing now, working as a program ambassador for a recovery community that's based in Los Angeles, Houston and New York, traveling around and simply telling young men and women my story. What they do with that is up to them.

My three ideals now are accountability, community and spirituality. It's like that old joke at Washington State. I once thought I was a god, but now I realize that I'm just a small part in all of this.

Sometimes, I wish I could carry somebody whose struggling 18 months down the line to see what a different perspective and a changed life is going to look like. But the daily struggle is what's going to make you stronger.

I was at the scouting combine in Indianapolis last week with a group the league calls "NFL Legends," and we were there to help players by talking to them. During introductions, the league starts rattling off the years that people played: <u>Mark Brunell</u>, 17 years. Tony Richardson, 16 years . . . Ryan Leaf, 5 years." Any time I do anything around the NFL, it kind of slams the ego back in place.

What you're doing is being of service to people, not being paraded around like you are this great thing. I was walking down the hall of the hotel and thinking, "I'm a tough SOB. I just keep getting back up, getting back up. That's what it's about.

"It's simply progress and not perfection. You're not going to be perfect. I was a certain way for 38 years. It's not going to change overnight. Hell, I might not figure it out until I'm 76. But one day I will.

My best thinking in my lifetime took me to a prison cell. So now I have what's essentially a board of directors, five guys that I go with to help me make significant decisions in my life. I'm the chairman, and I ultimately make the decision, but I generally go with what they say. And it has served me well, because every day I struggle with ego, narcissism, all those behaviors that existed long before the drug addiction.

These days, I do things completely different. I go to meetings. I meditate. I pray. I see a therapist every other week. I'm coming up on 5 years since I went to prison, and it doesn't matter. It's just about today.

Thursdays are my favorite days. I get up at 6, I'm in the gym at 7, and I'm in the office from about 9 until 1 p.m. Then, I'm back to the gym for a program that works with former combat vets. I'm home around 5 p.m. with my fiancé and our little dog. You know, that's a boring life. And boring is not a bad word anymore." (Farmer, 2017)

Today Ryan's life has even more meaning. He is a father and husband and travels all over the country talking with others about his journey. His new life of service and redemption has opened doors that perhaps at one point in his life he never thought would open again. He is a radio host and PAC-12 Network Analyst, just to name a few. Leaf on Twitter has 42,000 followers. His followers, for the most part, are supportive but he still takes an occasional beating from haters on social media. The old Ryan Leaf may not have reacted the way the new one does. The new Ryan Leaf is more humble, gentle, and thoughtful, if you will. I messaged him on Twitter once and asked him if there was a daily affirmation he lives by. He gave me this famous Mark Twain quote. "What other people think of me is none of my business." He's right. When you are doing all you can to better yourself, and you are not hurting anyone in the process, it does not matter what anyone else says or thinks.

Keep making a difference in the lives of others Ryan! You have many people rooting for you, including us!

Formula for Success

The key for anyone that has a reputation to repair is what happens *after* the damage is done. Once again, we applied the ABCD method. Exercising these principles, whether you are an individual or a business, will set you on the road to recovery much quicker than doing nothing at all.

Apologize and Be Authentic

Be quick and be genuine. The longer you wait to apologize the less sincere it will seem and your motives will be perceived as questionable. Simply saying, "I'm sorry" is not enough. People do not forgive easily, so you will have to be patient. Forgiveness takes time, and we must be humble as we patiently wait. And leave the "if" out. The "if" is used to make an inauthentic apology—"I'm sorry *if* I offended anyone." That completely takes away any admission of guilt on the part of the person "apologizing."

Behave

Continue to behave like the person you want to be until you *become* that person. Remember that your reputation stems from both what you *say* and what you *do*. Do not rationalize your past behavior. Reestablish trust in yourself through repetitive actions that demonstrate that you are trustworthy again.

Come Clean and Commit to Change

Do not just talk the talk. Start by taking action. Do what you say you are going do. Clearly communicate your commitment to long-term change. Be transparent, be decisive, and be fast in correcting your behavior.

Deliberately Move Forward

Look deep within and figure out how you landed in this situation in the first place. Then learn to forgive yourself. Seek professional help from people who will give you tools to change. This might be a good time to go back and revisit your values.

> "Do not leave your reputation to chance or gossip; it is your life's artwork, and you must craft it, hone, and display it with the care of an artist."
> —Robert Greene

Before we wrap up this chapter we do want to update you on Justine Sacco, the public relations executive who carelessly tweeted her way out of a job and smeared her reputation by writing "Going to South Africa. Hope I don't get AIDS. Just Kidding I'm white!"

After losing her job at IAC, she went to Ethiopia for a month where she volunteered for a nonprofit organization doing public relations work. Once back in New York she gained employment at a couple of other online PR companies. Just last year Sacco landed back at the former firm that previously fired her, IAC. Joey Levin, CEO of IAC and chairman of Match Group, shared a statement with Recode, an online daily tech and business newsletter: "With one notable exception, Justine's track record speaks for itself. Very few people in the business world have Justine's indomitable spirit, tenacity and drive to persevere. That's the kind of talent we seek. I'm happy to have her great mind and boundless positive energy back on the team." (Wagner, 2018) We think it is safe to say she has learned some valuable lessons to carry into her future.

So yes, people do mess up. You and I are probably going to mess up, too. How we handle the aftermath matters the most. Let us hope we can all learn from our mistakes and the mistakes of others. Otherwise, we have missed the valuable lessons we could have learned from them.

Bottom line: We are all worth more than second chances. If you find your reputation in need of repair, commit to change. We have the ability to apologize and move forward. Shame has a way of paralyzing us. Do not live with shame. Learn from it as you continue to sharpen your **Reputation by Design**.

Activity for Repairing Your Reputation

If I Could Have a "Do-Over"

This is an intrapersonal activity that you may choose to keep completely to yourself. Dig deep into your past, near past, or very long ago past. Think of something that you did that you are not proud of or are embarrassed about.

You messed up, just like the rest of us. We all do. Sure, you would probably like to just forget about it. Remember the old saying, "We can learn from our mistakes?" Perhaps if you take some time to revisit the scenario and replay it with a different ending, you, too, can learn from your mistake.

In the space below, briefly tell your story about "what happened."

_____

_____

_____

_____

_____

_____

Now, knowing what you know about repairing your reputation, rewrite your story, only with a different ending. Write it with the ending you would like now if you had a "do-over."

_____

_____

_____

_____

_____

_____

Hopefully, you will now have the tools in your toolbox to think about your actions ahead of time and realize how you can take steps to keep your reputation strong.

References

Farmer, S. (2017, March 12). Los Angeles Times, Copyright © 2017 by Los Angeles Times. Reprinted by permission.

McKinnon, J. D. (2019, April 5). *Americans hate social media but can't give it up, WSJ/NBC news poll finds.* Retrieved from https://www.wsj.com/articles/americans-agree-social-media-is-divisive-but-we-keep-using-it-11554456600

Olivia Jade previously revealed her parents warned that "you only get one reputation" (n.d.). Retrieved from https://www.msn.com/en-us/tv/celebrity/olivia-jade-previously-revealed-her-parents-warned-that-you-only-get-one-reputation/ar-BBVDvFq

Wagner, K. (2018, January 19). *Justine Sacco, the PR exec who was fired from IAC for her tweets, has landed back at IAC's Match Group.* Retrieved from https://www.recode.net/2018/1/19/16911074/justine-sacco-iac-match-group-return-tweet

When good role models go bad. (2019, March 22). Retrieved from http://www.spokesman.com/stories/2019/mar/23/when-good-role-models-go-bad

chapter 6

DIS(CONNECT)

Imagine yourself living a long, healthy, happy, and successful life filled with a number of great friends. You are living a life without anxiety, loneliness, or depression. You are filled with self-confidence and living with a sense of purpose.

> We were put on this universe to serve more than just ourselves.

If we told you it would only take *one* thing on your part to achieve this…would you do it? Most people reading this would say "yes," but very few would actually follow through. We are talking about volunteering. Studies have linked a long list of benefits when it comes to doing something good for *others*. What if you took the hours of screen time you *use* daily and apply them to the hours you *choose* to serve those in need? The world would be a much better place in which to live.

By helping others…
…we help ourselves

My 98-year-old grandma once told me, "I spend my days helping others so I don't have to think about my own aches and pains." She has donated many hours of her life quilting for the homeless and volunteering for hospice. It is no wonder when her house burned to the ground in the Paradise, California fires that she had so many people offering to help her pick up the pieces and began donating back to her.

"Volunteering helps counteract the effects of stress, anger, and anxiety. The social contact aspect of helping and working with others can have a profound effect on your overall psychological well-being. Nothing relieves stress better than a meaningful connection to another person." ("Volunteering and its surprising benefits")

I have worked for the same television station, KHQ TV, as an anchor/reporter for the past 22 years. When anyone asks me what the secret to my success is, I tell them this: I'm not the smartest, prettiest, thinnest, or best anchor out there. The secret to my longevity is that I got involved with my community and I chipped in to help make a difference in the lives of others. I have spent countless hours volunteering my time to organizations so others in our community can get the help they need during difficult times. I worked to become part of a solution, and in the process, it changed who I am as a person. In turn, I know the people I serve trust me. This has filled my heart, connected me to my community, and has given my life

NO ONE has ever become **poor** from giving

© www.subtropica/Shutterstock.com

deeper meaning. Even when my career as a journalist comes to a close I know one thing: I will always be of service to others, and I thank my company for teaching me the value of volunteering. Volunteering humbles you and makes you more appreciative of the life you have. Very rarely do I complain during difficult times because I have learned that things can always be much worse.

My coanchor and several friends have started their own nonprofits to help veterans, the elderly, terminally ill, and the less fortunate in our region. I can hear the humility in their voices when they talk about helping those who may not have long to live, or they may suffer with post-traumatic stress disorder (PTSD), or live with disabilities, or without resources they so desperately need.

"Volunteering is knowledge that helps you understand the challenges others face and to appreciate the obstacles

Source: Donna Kleckner

they have conquered. For me, helping those who have served our country brings a sense of pride I couldn't find anywhere else."—Dan Kleckner

No Time, No Problem

Volunteering does not have to take a lot of your time. Many are just grateful for any time, or donation, you are willing to give. If I do not have time I make it a

© Mila Supinskaya Glashchenko/Shutterstock.com

point to donate. Giving is easy and it not only helps those who need it most, it improves *your* happiness and health at the same time. I have a rule: I will not buy a new article of clothing until I donate a piece of clothing first.

When Passion Meets Purpose

Before signing up to volunteer, think about your passions. Do you get heated up when talking about animal cruelty, child abuse, domestic violence, homelessness, cancer, global warming? Just about anything that makes your blood boil is a good indicator it means something to you. Align yourself with an organization you would be interested in helping out. Otherwise, unless you want to learn something new, you may not get the experience you were hoping for.

Volunteer to Make a Difference

Think about the talents you can bring to the organization. If you like what you are doing, chances are you will be supporting them for a while. My grandma loved quilting. To think she gave comfort to people with no shelter at night or were living their last moments in hospices warms my heart to this day.

Photo taken by Annafelia Tillman

"Volunteering saves lives, both the lives of the people you help and yours. When you invest the time and energy to volunteer, you are investing in yourself just as much as in the causes you support." ("15 reasons to get off the couch and volunteer")

Bottom line: The act of service to others is a great way to build a respectable *Reputation by Design*. It shows people you are thoughtful, giving, and willing to pitch in when help is needed. It looks great on a resume and impresses future employers who are looking for a well-rounded person to hire. We all love team players!

Tips To Get You Started

Ask yourself these questions to narrow down a choice.

Do I want to . . .

. . . expand my circle of friends?

. . . meet new people in my community?

. . . do something new with my spare time?

. . . do more with my hobbies and interests?

. . . share a unique talent I have?

. . . try something new?

. . . see a different side of life?

. . . see if I want to work in a career field like this?

These points should help you narrow down your search.

Try this:

Think about social causes that you are passionate about. For example, feeding the hungry, sheltering the homeless, sustainability . . . you get the idea.

Now let us do some research. Seek out organizations in your local community that could use volunteers. Call them and ask them questions about their needs. Think about how much time you can commit and take the next step. Think about how good you will feel helping others and serving in your community.

References

Fritz, J. (n.d.). *15 reasons to get off the couch and volunteer*. Retrieved from https://www.thebalancesmb.com/unexpected-benefits-of-volunteering-4132453

Volunteering and its surprising benefits. (2019, March 28). Retrieved from https://www.helpguide.org/articles/healthy-living/volunteering-and-its-surprising-benefits.htm

chapter 7

THANK YOU!

A Simple Note Can Change Your Life!

You dreaded taking the time to sit down and do it, but your mom insisted. You may not want to hear this but mom was right... again! The impression you leave by expressing your gratitude goes a long way in life. Sure it started with a two-sentence thank you note to your grandparents after Christmas, but eventually it will be someone who may hold the key to your future.

© Huhehoda/Shutterstock.com

Stand Out From the Rest!

© mcherevan/Shutterstock.com

Life is busy. People are busy. You make not think it matters or that anyone will notice the tiny piece of paper that comes in the mail, but that 3" × 4" card shows you took time to acknowledge someone for doing something they did not necessarily have to. Showing gratitude is the fastest way to build your credibility and reputation. People appreciate kind and thoughtful people.

When it comes down to making a decision to choose a possible candidate for a job, the one that sends a thank you note is typically the one that gets picked. As a matter of fact, it is likely that you will be dismissed as a potential candidate if you do not follow up with a note of gratitude. "It is important to understand the value of time. A company will spend hundreds of dollars in time interviewing a candidate. A candidate that does not show gratitude and appreciation for that time is someone I am not initially interested in hiring," says Jeff Kavidias CPA, partner of the accounting firm, Kavadias Hall PLLC. Many people, like Jeff, feel the same way about those who do not take the time to say thank you. It shows that you really do not care about the kindness that was just extended to you. It is not enough to say I was too busy to do it, because nowadays everyone seems "too busy."

Is an E-Mail or Text Ok?

We know that the platforms for sending and receiving thank you messages have shifted over the years. Our own children have been known to thank their aunts, uncles, and grandparents via Facebook or Facebook Messenger, but we believe to stand out above the rest the best way still is the traditional hand-written thank you note. The note itself demonstrates intention and effort on your part. A lot of people enjoy displaying their note of thanks because it feels good to be recognized for their kindness, especially when it comes from a thoughtful YOU!

When Should I Write a Thank You?

ASAP or as soon as possible! The longer you wait to write a thank you note the more likely it is that you will forget to do it. The sooner you send it the faster it will get there and the bigger the impression that you will leave. This is especially important if you want to land a job. The message you are sending is that you are a person that is on top of your game.

Personalize Your Message

It is no secret that showing gratitude not only strengthens relationships, but also reinforces positive behavior. If you know someone appreciates your gift, your time, your effort, or your care, it is likely that you will be more inclined to repeat the behavior in the future. Let's face it—a genuine compliment or sincere thank you note also boosts your self-esteem.

Many of my students have asked me to write letters of reference for them over the years, and

I am always so impressed with the ones who take the time to write a note of thanks. It says that they value what I have done for them, and it is also more likely that I will remember them down the road if they need another reference.

Only for You!

Personalize the note by remembering something important from your time together. It makes my heart happy when I get e-mails out of the blue from former students which describe how a particular course that I taught them has come in handy or benefited them. Here is one example of an "unexpected" thank-you" e-mail I received:

gratitude is the best attitude

© Courtney Johnson/Shutterstock.com

> Hi Professor McMahon,
>
> I hope all is well with you at Gonzaga and you are enjoying your summer!!
>
> I moved to Boston a couple of weeks ago for a sales position with Dell. I have been going through a new-hire training program that is one of the more difficult things I have done. Your speech class has helped me significantly do better than my peers when it comes to articulating ideas and giving presentations on our technology. For that, I wanted to say thank you!! Even though those pennies in the jar were intimidating, they made me a better speaker.
>
> Again, thank you!
> Madi

She didn't just say, "Thank you for your class" or "for teaching me." She got specific about what was helpful for her.

You Never Climb the Ladder Alone

"Don't ever forget the people, experiences and places that got you where you are today. Every step, every bump, it all got you to where you are today. Try to appreciate that," says Emmy Award winning journalist, Hayley Guenthner. Successful people did not get to the top without help from others. Maybe someone took a chance on you and hired you for a position that you were not fully qualified for. Maybe someone took you under his or her wing and mentored you when you were younger. Now, fast forward. You are enjoying a new career and feeling rather successful. That person who took the chance on you or mentored you would absolutely love to know that to this day you appreciate what he or she did for you, even if it was a very long time ago. Letting people who have helped you achieve success know that they are appreciated can go a long way in reinforcing personal and professional relationships. It's all about connections.

© GUGAI/Shutterstock.com

"For years I'd send my first News Director a Christmas photo of my sons and me. After I left the station I wanted him to know I felt forever indebted because he took a chance on me. One day while looking through old newspaper clippings I came across an article about me after he'd given me a huge promotion. His words about me in that article were so kind that it really tugged at my heartstrings. I was so touched that I sent him a Facebook message that went like this:

Every time you cross my mind... I smile! Thank you for giving me the opportunity to live my dream. I've been in this crazy business for 24 years now. You taught me so much. You changed my life for the better.

God bless you and your family Sanders.

Fondly, Stephanie Vigil

© anaken2012/Shutterstock.com

Two days later I read that my former boss, Jim Sanders, passed away. I am so happy I sent that message. It reaffirmed for me the importance of letting people know how much they are appreciated.

Where Do I Start?

If you are not in the habit of writing thank you notes, do not fear. You are in luck. We will give you specific tips and demonstrations on how to write a succinct, sincere, and effective note of thanks. We have even included a thank you note and envelope for you to use!

How to Write a Thank You Note

Start with the greeting. It is pretty straightforward. Start with "Dear" and the person's name followed by a comma. And by all means, make absolutely sure you are spelling the person's name correctly. *Dear Aunt Betty,* The next line is where you get right to the point and say thank you for whatever it is that he or she gave you or did for you. *Thank you for the lovely green shirt.* Then you might say something about that gift that means a lot to you or what you really like about it. *How did you know that was my favorite color?* Next, you might add another personal note. *I will think of you every time I wear it.* Finally, thank him or her again. *Again, thank you for the thoughtful gift.* And then you want to end with your regards. *Many thanks, With love, Yours truly,* followed by your name. All together it looks like this:

Dear Aunt Betty,

Thank you for the lovely green shirt. How did you know that was my favorite color? I will think of you every time I wear it. Thank you again for your thoughtfulness.

Yours truly,
Colleen

It does not need to be long to make your point. The one above was four sentences and probably would take less than 5 minutes to write. All you have left to do is to address the envelope with your return address on the upper left hand corner and the receiver's name and address in the middle of the envelope. It looks like this:

John Smith
222 Front Street,
Your city, State, 55555

        Betty Jones
        1234 Big Road Ave
        Her city, State, 88888

While the phrase "thank you" can sometimes feel trite or perhaps overused, making use of other ways to say it may come across as more authentic and sincere.

You can say, "I'm grateful," or "I'm grateful for the extra effort you put in on that project for me." Getting specific about *what* you are grateful for can go a long way. If you tell the person in a sentence or two what he or she has done that you appreciate, rather than, "Good job" (which can feel like a simple pat on the back), you demonstrate authenticity. When you overdo it, it can feel forced and insincere.

Bottom line: If you take only one piece of advice from this book, we hope it is this one. Making Thank You notes a part of your ritual will open so many doors in your life. You will stand out from the rest because it is obvious you are creating a **Reputation by Design**.

Do this:

Using the notepaper and envelope provided at the end of this chapter, write a thank you note to someone in your life who may not expect to receive it. Brainstorm for a few minutes about whom you might want to thank and why. Perhaps someone has always been your biggest cheerleader or "always been there for you." Perhaps they have helped you accomplish a personal goal. Perhaps they simply lent a listening ear when you really needed it. Or perhaps they helped you out of a jamb when you were stuck. There are numerous reasons for us to thank the people in our lives who have meant something to us along the way. Write a thank you note using the techniques we have described in this chapter—be specific and most importantly, be sincere. And make sure you properly address the envelope, put a stamp on it, and mail it. Do not delay. No doubt, you will make someone's day!

chapter 8

SAY WHAT???

You want a text. I would like a phone call. He insists on Snapchat. She wants to Face Time. The boss definitely prefers an e-mail. The more tools we use to communicate, the more chances we have to get it right . . . or wrong. How do we keep up with the changing ways to converse with one another so everyone can be heard?

Knowing how someone likes to communicate is the fastest way to develop a great reputation. There are several different generations in

the workplace these days. Each one has a preferred way of communicating. Even our own parents and grandparents appreciate a visit or phone call, while our children and the younger generation prefer to text.

A good communicator thinks of others first and they honor the basic principles of active listening, speaking, and writing.

Active Listening

Listening to the needs of others is what great leaders do. It is a skill not many people practice. There is a big difference between hearing and listening. The meaning of listening is that you are actively paying attention to the words and ideas that someone else is communicating. Hearing simply means that you have detected sounds, but are not necessarily focusing on the meaning. You hear background noises, you hear voices in a crowded party, but you do not necessarily focus specifically on what is being said.

As an active listener, you put in effort to *understand* what the other person is saying. You try to eliminate other distractions. It is so easy to be a passive listener these days because we find ourselves "multitasking" while we are in the company of others. Have you ever tried to have a conversation with people who do not seem to want to put down their phone? They pretend to be listening (they may nod their heads, say the occasional, "uh-huh,") but then when you ask them for feedback they may end up asking you to repeat what you said. If you truly want to be an active listener, and have a reputation for being attentive to others, put down your phone, make eye contact, and truly pay attention to what the other person is saying.

A genuine form of active listening is what we call *empathic listening*. As a leader, this is especially important. Your listening goal is to *understand* the other person and to try to "feel" the way the other person feels. You make a point to really understand his or her disappointment, frustrations, sadness, or other emotions he or she may be feeling. Your goal is to honestly appreciate the perspective of the other person without offering advice or judgment. Wouldn't we all like to have a reputation for being an authentically active listener?

EVERY GOOD CONVERSATION STARTS WITH GOOD LISTENING.

Speaking Successfully

Studies show that the higher you climb the "corporate ladder," the more opportunities you will have to give presentations. Since most of us do not aspire to stay at the bottom rung, the more you can learn about writing and delivering effective presentations, the more successful you will be. The more successful you are, the better your chances for enhancing your reputation. Whether you are a student, professional, or aspiring leader, there will always be opportunities to speak in public.

Part of being a strong leader is being a good speaker. If you think about it, some of the greatest leaders are also some of the strongest public speakers you have ever heard. Their ability to convey a powerful, convincing, and motivating message is a big reason why they achieved notoriety

to fame in the first place. For example, we are all familiar with the famous "I Have a Dream" speech by Martin Luther King, Jr. Do you think he would be mentioned as much in history if he had not delivered that memorable message? He earned a reputation as a powerful speaker.

Public Speaking

No other communication skill is as essential in our society as that of being an effective public speaker. Yet, most people receive either no instruction or minimal instruction in this area. You might think that because we spend so much time using mobile devices, e-mail, and social media, the art of public speaking is dying. It is not. Successful people will speak to large crowds often throughout their careers. Why not aspire to advance and be confident and effective at the same time? Designing your own reputation as a polished speaker is a smart goal!

Public speaking is not just giving a speech; public speaking is speaking in any situation that is beyond the comfort of our own homes!

© Photographee.eu/Shutterstock.com

Public speaking skills also come in quite handy in an interview setting. Yes, you are the center of attention, which can be a bit unnerving, but if you can become self-assured in an interview setting you are likely to become more comfortable with larger audiences. Adding public speaking to your list of qualifications will also be a *BIG* confidence booster.

Many successful leaders have had hours of training and coaching to help them overcome their fears and become powerful presenters. Fear is the number one reason people avoid public speaking, so let us take a look at what causes the fear and more importantly, what we can do about it.

Say you have been asked to make a presentation. What happens next? Do you panic? Most likely many of us will. As a matter of fact, many people will admit that they fake they are sick just to get out of giving a presentation! I know many of my students have done so.

If you are nervous, you are not alone. "You've probably heard that what people *fear the most* is speaking before a group, according to the *Book of Lists*. Public speaking is feared more than even snakes or death. Now that does not necessarily mean that people would rather die than give a speech! It simply points out that the fear of public speaking is a common phenomenon." (McMahon & Prindle, 2015)

> "The best way to conquer public speaking fear is to know what you're talking about."
> —Michael H. Mescon

Public speaking fear or "stage fright" shows up in both psychological and physical ways. We may be thinking about all the things that could go wrong and naturally, we become stressed. Then the very thought of giving a presentation makes us feel jittery, or even possibly "sick." Part of the reason is that most of us have a natural desire to be liked, respected, and approved. This is quite normal as long as we do not take it to an extreme. Before we give you tips on how to avoid feeling this way, let us talk about how public speaking fear plays out physically on our bodies.

Have you ever paid attention to what happens to you, physically, when you panic or something startles you? "For example, have you ever driven on ice? No matter what you try to do, such as pumping your brakes or attempting to steer in a different direction, the car seems to have a mind of its own. As a result, our stress mechanism kicks in and we may start shaking, we may perspire, we may break out in hives, or experience some other unpleasant physiological reaction. These physical—or stress—reactions are often beyond our control." (McMahon & Prindle, 2015)

That stress can either be positive or negative. When it is negative we stay fearful for a long time and it takes over. And there is no way we will ever feel comfortable speaking up. On the other hand, when the stress is "positive" it can help the nervous speaker actually become better prepared and more focused. Positive stress comes from excitement and anticipation—typically something we are really looking forward to, and have made sure we are totally ready. Learn to embrace the opportunity, and talk to yourself in a positive way.

Preparation Is Key

Preparation is key to reducing your fear of speaking in front of a group. The more you have carefully crafted and practiced your presentation the more at ease you will be when it comes time to present. Do NOT expect to just wing it. Very few of us can get away with it. You will not fool your audience either. There is a direct correlation between lack of preparation and anxiety. The less prepared you are, the more anxious you will feel, and in turn, the less effective your presentation will be. A reputation as someone who has strong public speaking skills can be your gateway to success!

PROOFREAD
☑ Spelling
☑ Grammar
☑ Accuracy

Getting It Write

Bad writing can ruin your professional reputation. I have been known to tell my students, "Every time you write something and send it

> "Your grammar is a reflection of your image. Good or bad, you have made an impression. And like all impressions, you are in total control"
> —Jeffrey Gitomer

to another person to read, and it has your name on it, it's a reflection of you and/or your organization." It can say so many things without you actually "saying" anything. Just as easily as you can be perceived as lacking credibility, careless, or impulsive, you can be perceived as being credible, thoughtful, and thorough.

There are so many useful tools available to help us be better writers, double-check our spelling and grammar, and send clear, concise messages, but so often we do not take the time to do that. We are busy and we are inundated with tons of messages each day. Whether you are writing a paper for school or replying to a colleague's e-mail, it is crucial for the sake of your own reputation to make sure you are sending out error-free messages.

One technique that has worked well for many of my students is to read what you have written *out loud, and slowly*. If you have trouble catching your own writing errors you are not alone. Even though we *see* the grammar or spelling error we read over it because it *sounds* right to us. We do not catch our own errors because we know the *meaning* of what we are trying to say. We *expect* what we *meant* to be there. It does not matter how smart you are, it happens to all of us. It is much easier to catch someone else's errors because you are not the one creating the meaning.

If you know that proofreading is a challenge for you, I recommend that you get a second set of eyes. The last thing you want to have happen is for someone to read what you have written and dismiss it outright because your grammar, style, or punctuation errors distracted him/her.

Communicate clearly, eliminate confusion, and accurately present your ideas. Ease the reader's task. And remember your A, B, Cs:

Accuracy—Make sure you have checked every fact, number, and claim. No grammar, spelling, or punctuation errors.

Brevity—Get to the point! Your writing gets stronger with each unnecessary word removed.

Clarity—It must make sense to the reader. If you can, do show what you have written to someone not familiar with your topic and get feedback.

© kpatyhka/Shutterstock.com

Write tight! Make sure every word means what you intend it to mean. The hallmark of great writing is simplicity and clarity, not fancy language. Write in shorter sentences using active verbs. Forget the BIG words. You want to have a reputation of being a clear communicator.

We have many ways to put our words in writing these days, but one way that we communicate frequently is via e-mail. Let us talk about e-mail etiquette.

"Your e-mail is a reflection of you. Every e-mail you send adds to, or detracts from your reputation. If your e-mail is scattered, disorganized, and filled with mistakes, the recipient will be inclined to think of you as a scattered, careless, and disorganized businessperson. Other people's opinions matter and in the professional world, their perception of you will be critical to your success."—Peter Post, director of the Burlington, Vermont-based Emily Post Institute, which offers etiquette advice and answers to manners questions such as wedding etiquette, parenting issues and table manners. ("25 tips for perfecting your e-mail etiquette")

I cannot tell you how many e-mails I have received from students with no SUBJECT in the subject line. Then, they address me as, "Hey." Wow. What a way to get my attention. If you are addressing someone in what should be a formal e-mail, you should begin with "Dear Mr. or Mrs. or Ms. or Dr. So and So." You should always use the person's title, name, and last name, for example, *Dear Professor Smith*. If you cannot find a formal title for the person you are addressing, it is perfectly appropriate to address a man as "Dear Mr." or a female as "Dear Ms." There are also appropriate ways to sign off on an e-mail. We suggest, "Best," "Regards," "Kind regards," or "Sincerely," "Yours truly," suggests a more intimate relationship and would be inappropriate.

The next part of your message you need to be careful with is your tone. Are you demanding? Do you leave the recipient wondering what exactly you want? As we talked about earlier in this chapter, you need to be direct. You need to make sure you phrase your request respectfully. For example, if you want to make an appointment with your professor you can do one of two things. You can say, "I want to make an appointment with you." Or, more appropriately, you can say, "Do you have time to meet with me sometime this week?" If you need to reschedule an appointment, instead of saying, "I need to reschedule our appointment" you can say, "Is it possible to reschedule?" This is common courtesy.

Always, before you hit send, do the following:

Check to make sure you spelled the recipient's name properly. And do not abbreviate the person's name until invited to do so. For example, do not address "Patrick" as "Pat," unless he gives you permission.

Make sure you read the e-mail thoroughly and answer the question that was asked. If you do not respond to a question or ask questions that were answered in a previous e-mail it appears that you have not taken the time to read the e-mail. That does not make you look good. Also, avoid ALL CAPS if possible. They are so hard to interpret. Are you excited? Are you yelling? If someone does not know you well enough it can really send a conversation off the rails.

Exclamation marks!!!! In an academic or professional e-mail, you want to avoid exclamation marks because they can be misinterpreted as angry, immature or too enthusiastic. Exceptions can be made when you are praising someone (great job!).

If you have sent your e-mail late in the day, do not expect an immediate response. Remember, many people do not check their professional e-mail accounts on their personal time.

You Can Never Erase the Written Word

That is why being thoughtful in your texts, posts, e-mails, and tweets should be at the top of your priority list. The effects of an offensive statement can cost you friends, jobs, and perhaps even legal trouble. Do not post impulsively or when you have extremely strong feelings. As Professional Educational Coach, Farrah Parker, MA, says, "Take the safe road and post as though your most critical opponent is watching." ("How your reputation impacts your career in psychology")

© Wor Sang Jun/Shutterstock.com

Do Not Let Lazy Be Your Excuse

Everyone is in a rush these days, but do not be too busy to take care of the little things, because little things can often make the biggest differences. *We take short cuts w our words bc it's faster when we txt.* But acronyms and abbreviations can be confusing. Lately I have noticed people are too busy to even put a period at the end of their sentences when messaging me. I am sure your friends are fine with it, but it is a bad habit to develop.

Bottom line: Challenge yourself to be an effective communicator because there are so many rewards by doing so. People who are great communicators are highly regarded as competent, reliable, and concise. Practice clear communication often and you will be enjoying the many benefits of your **Reputation by Design**.

Great Communicators . . . .

. . . are honest.

. . . establish a connection.

. . . seek understanding.

. . . are great listeners.

. . . ask good questions.

. . . respond to others in a timely manner.

. . . make eye contact at least **75%** of the time.

. . . are aware of what their body language is saying.

Try this:

Practice Active Listening

Find a partner for this exercise. If you are in a class break into pairs. The first person should spend approximately 2 minutes telling the other person about one of the most difficult things he or she ever had to do. The second person should practice empathic listening. The goal is to listen while focusing on the meaning the speaker is communicating. The listener should not interrupt at all or provide feedback. When the first person has finished the story, the second person should paraphrase back to the speaker what he or she heard. The listener should describe the feelings that he or she perceived that the speaker was feeling as the story was told. Then reverse the process. When both have told their stories and received feedback, discuss how accurate the listener's perceptions were. How hard was it to listen without wanting to give feedback? We all listen with the intent to respond, but if you listen to *understand,* you will be an empathic listener.

Do this:

Create Your Elevator Pitch

Most of us, at some time or another, will find ourselves in a job interview or a potential networking situation where someone will ask you to "tell me about yourself." Would you know what to say? Would you be able to respond succinctly, as opposed to rambling and scrambling for the right words? A handy tool to have "in your back pocket" is an Elevator Pitch. A good Elevator Pitch is anywhere from 30 to 60 seconds. No longer. In both speaking and writing, brevity is the key. In the space below, create your own Elevator Pitch and commit it to memory so the next time you are asked you will be ready to sell yourself convincingly. Begin by thinking about your career or internship goal that you are seeking. Then tailor your pitch to that end. Describe your skills and qualities that align with your goal. Briefly describe any experience you have that would be valuable to the job or internship that you desire. Speaking in terms of things you have accomplished or visible results of those accomplishments will enhance your pitch. Finally, make sure you end with a call to action. Ask for a coffee date to further discuss your credentials or a follow-up meeting to learn more about the other person's organization. While many of us may find it difficult to "toot our own horns," if you don't, who will? Write your Elevator Pitch and practice it for someone who will give you honest feedback. Once it is in its final form, commit it to memory, but practice it so you sound naturally conversational, not memorized.

Hi, my name is_____

_____

_____

_____

_____

_____

_____

_____

_____

_____

_____

_____

Give this a try:

Netiquette Assignment

"Netiquette" means Internet etiquette. Please review the section in this chapter on writing an effective e-mail and do the following:

Write a short e-mail to an employer, organization, or graduate school *requesting more information. You are not requesting an interview, but more information* about the company, a position, etc. This exercise will help you practice sending out a formal e-mail.

The purpose of the e-mail is to get you thinking about communicating professionally *electronically.* This is a *formal* e-mail, so you will also get practice in sending important information electronically. Often, people send informal e-mails addressing formal matters. Always know your audience. Proofread carefully before you send the e-mail.

References

How your reputation impacts your career in psychology. (n.d.). Retrieved from https://careersinpsychology.org/how-reputation-impacts-career-psychology

McMahon, C., & Prindle, R. (2015). *Speech writing and delivery for public relations*. Dubuque, IA: Kendall Hunt Publishing Company.

Silberman, L. (n.d.). *25 tips for perfecting your e-mail etiquette*. Retrieved from http://www.inc.com/guides/2010/06/email-etiquette.html?cid=readmoretextrev

chapter 9

SUCCESS STARTS HERE

A GOAL
WITHOUT A PLAN
IS JUST A WISH

© rosewind/Shutterstock.com

The most successful people do not find success by *wishing* for it. They become great at what they do because they *work* for it. They set up a game plan and they map out a course that will help them achieve their goal. "Successful people have lofty dreams, and they set long-term and short-term goals that will get them there. They write their goals down and work on them constantly. If you want to become successful, one of the easiest habits to develop is to start setting goals for yourself and create a plan of action to achieve those goals." (Patel, 2018) It is not easy to create new habits, but it is necessary if you want change.

> "Set lofty goals, ask for help, learn from peers and those who have succeeded before you. Have a mentor whom you respect unconditionally. Four words to live by: confidence, determination, education and most importantly trustworthiness."
> —Brooke M. Cloninger, D.D.S

So what is it that you want so badly in your life that you can taste it? Maybe it is a promotion at work, eating healthier, lowering your golf handicap, connecting more with your family, or getting your degree. All these goals are realistic and entirely possible if you start by making a commitment to state what it is that you want in life.

It takes time to sit down and map out a course of action, but we can guarantee it will be worth your time. "Goals provide clarity. We all know that when we have a clear vision or desire, taking the proper action is easier. When you have to put the pen to paper, only the truth comes out. Whatever is written becomes real." (McCracken, 2017)

It is important to have both personal and professional goals. This provides balance in our lives. It is good to have many passions in your life. That is what keeps it exciting!

It is amazing how many doors begin to open once you begin making a list of what is important to you. It is as if our mind subconsciously starts focusing on what it is we desire to do and be, and as we talk about them with others our world starts to open up. Just ask Dr. Cloninger. She has built a successful practice where she because she focused on her goals and she did not have just one goal, she had many.

© marekuliasz/
Shutterstock.com

The Day My Life Changed Forever

I wanted to be a television news reporter since I was a kid. I'm a very curious person and I love learning. While in college I listened to the advice of others and majored in business instead of journalism. Bad choice! I hated statistics. My very last semester I had an internship at a TV station in Sacramento, CA and quickly realized I should have followed my passion for journalism.

After graduation, I began working at a radio station selling commercials. I was the worst salesperson out there! That's when I knew if I wanted to be happy I had to change my professional path. It was then that I plotted my new course by writing down my goals. I went back to college, interned at **another** TV station, made a resume reel, made numerous phone calls and began bringing my resume to every station up and down northern California. I didn't just write all of those steps down, I put a date to them. I even got a job as a radio traffic reporter for a while. Gaining experience with my eye on the prize, I worked as hard as I could.

I wanted my dream job by February 15, 1994. I stayed focused and didn't let anything, or anyone, stand in my way. During my internship I asked questions, soaked up as much advice and information as possible, learned from seasoned veterans, dressed the part, and offered to do more than what was expected of me. The more I learned the more I could see myself getting one step closer to my goal. It was tough, and at times I felt defeated, but I was determined.

On February 14, 1994, one day before my goal date, I signed my very first contract as a television News Reporter for KOVR TV 13 in Sacramento. My news director, Jim Sanders said, "I have no choice but to hire you, because you won't go away." It was a day that changed my life forever in the best way possible!

Looking back, I can honestly say that I would have veered off course had it not been for my goals. My life has taken a lot of twists and turns, but my goals have kept me focused. It takes grit, a good work ethic and determination, but I promise, if you believe in yourself, set goals and work hard, you will achieve success.

–Stephanie

This business card was proof I had accomplished a significant goal in my life.

Fear and Doubt

Do not let fear and doubt creep in. Sometimes we let those two enemies get the best of us. It is normal to have both these emotions, but you cannot let them paralyze you. You can conquer fear and doubt by designing an action plan and arming yourself with knowledge. The more we know the less we are afraid.

We will all have setbacks in life. There will be people who say no, but that does not mean you should stop trying. As a matter of fact, let it motivate you to try

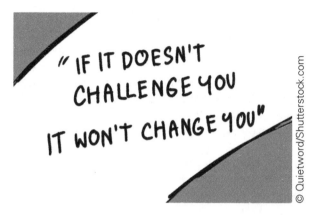

harder. You have to challenge yourself in order to change. Nothing worthwhile comes easy. Confidence builds when you accomplish your goals. We do not think you can do it, we KNOW you can!

Accountability Is Key

One key to achieving your goals is to be accountable. Do not think of accountability as a negative thing, like feeling that you have to report or answer to someone. That makes accountability sound like a weight around your ankle. Think of it as giving yourself a gift and one more way for you to stay true to yourself.

One way to keep yourself accountable is to have a "goal buddy." Your authors do that when they have a personal goal to achieve (exercise, healthy eating, etc.). If you are a professional or have a supervisor, share your goal(s) with your boss to add another layer of accountability. If you are known for setting goals, and achieving them, you are strengthening your self-esteem and your reputation.

Be Flexible

Life happens. We change. What we valued one decade ago may not be what we value in the next. On occasion reevaluate your goals and give yourself the liberty to change them. Sometimes we need to recognize when things no longer make sense or work for our lives. Maybe it is time to ditch the old goal and start with something new. "Goals help you achieve your own personal success. Real success is knowing that no matter what happens tomorrow, you are still giving your best today." (McCracken, 2017)

YOU ARE NEVER TOO OLD TO SET ANOTHER GOAL OR TO DREAM A NEW DREAM

© Helen_st/Shutterstock.com

Track Your Progress

CREATE A VISION THAT MAKES YOU WANNA JUMP OUT OF BED IN THE MORNING.

© StudioByTheSea/Shutterstock.com

It gives you a way to "measure" your results and a way of knowing when you have achieved success. You can visually see the steps you have taken and the ones you still need to take. Keep a list of your goals handy (maybe by your nightstand) and look at them often, working toward them day after day, month after month. Visualize yourself achieving them one step at a time with a deadline attached.

Let Us Put a Plan Together!

We can talk about it until we are blue in the face, but let us work on it together, right now. Sit for a while and write down things you would like to accomplish this week. I, personally, would like to make my bed every day so I have a fresh bed I can slip into every night. Why would this bring value to my life? I think my room will look nicer; my bed is pretty, and should look that way. I also think it reflects how chaotic my life can become when it is messy. When would I like to see this happen? Let us start with every day this week.

A long-term goal would be to compete in an Ironman Triathlon. That means I need to swim 2.4 miles, bike 112 miles, and complete a marathon, which is 26.22 miles, in less than 17 hours.

That is a lot of training so I need to start by coming up with weekly goals. I may need to hire a coach to help me shave time off my swim and my run. I will need to educate myself on some new techniques for every leg of the course. I need to watch videos on eating properly so my body efficiently burns calories while training, and I need to learn how to replenish myself with the right food.

I like this goal because I love the feeling of crossing finish lines. The value this brings me is the pride I feel knowing that I have pushed my body harder than I ever knew I could. There are many steps I will need to take to get me there, but I do believe I can accomplish this goal 1 year from now.

What do YOU want? Dream big, write it down, take those steps to make your dreams a reality. Use the following pages to get you started. If you need more pages, they will be in the back of the book.

> "Whatever you think you can do or believe you can do, begin it. Action has magic, grace and power in it."
> —Johann Wolfgang von Goethe

Bottom Line: Goals get you excited because achieving success feels good! Goals also add value to your life and your credibility. Stay focused on your goals, and get excited about the little steps that you accomplish along the way. Goal-oriented people are admired for their motivation. By making yourself a priority, and taking charge of your life, you are creating a ***Reputation by Design***.

Goal	Value	Action	Date

Goal	Value	Action	Date

Goals Are Good for You!

Goals should be realistic.

Goals should be both long and short term.

Goals are measurable.

Goals keep you focused.

Goals keep you on a path.

Goals help you develop good habits.

Goals keep you from procrastinating.

Goals keep you motivated.

GREAT THINGS **NEVER** *came from* **COMFORT ZONES**

© TheSaif/Shutterstock.com

FAILURE IS NOT THE OPPOSITE OF SUCCESS. IT IS PART OF SUCCESS.

© happydancing/Shutterstock.com

Goals Activity:

What's My Motive?

Think of a personal goal you would like to accomplish. No matter how big or small, think about why you want to accomplish this goal.

What is motivating you to want to accomplish this goal?_____

_____

_____

_____

Why is it important to you?_____

_____

_____

Please be very honest with yourself. Are you hoping to accomplish this goal for yourself or to please someone else? Sometimes it's perfectly fine to want to improve or change something about yourself for the benefit of a relationship you have with another person.

_____

_____

_____

What is going to keep you motivated toward achieving your goal when you may not feel like continuing? _____

_____

_____

_____

Find an *inspiring quote* and put it here and on a big piece of paper that you can see often that is going to help you keep your eye on the prize. _____

_____

_____

_____

Come back to this page often as you continue on your journey to accomplish your goal. And remember: You Got This!!!

References

McCracken, M. (2017, November 21). *The real reason setting goals is so critical to success.* Retrieved from https://www.inc.com/mareo-mccracken/the-real-reason-setting-goals-is-so-critical-to-success.html

Patel, D. (2018, September 5). *10 powerful attributes of insanely successful people.* Retrieved from https://www.entrepreneur.com/article/319058

chapter 10

FINAL THOUGHTS

We know chances are very slim that you will practice all that we have written in this book, but we hope you will at least try a couple of exercises that have had lasting impressions on us.

It is the tiny little tweaks in your life that can lead to substantial changes over time. You create a habit and eventually your habit will create the "you" that you want to be!

In the beginning of this book, we asked you to write down the words that describe the person you admire the most in your life. How many of those words are words that people would use to describe you? Follow in the path of your role model and you will likely become admired in just the same way.

For those entering the professional world, think about these statistics: "Of the 250 resumes going out for every corporate job, the initial screening typically eliminates 98 percent of job seekers, and only 2 percent will even get the interview," according to Gary Burnison, CEO of Korn Ferry. ("Skills gap? what skills gap?") We want you to be the one that lands your dream job!

When it comes to your work-life balance, we offer this advice to our own children and to our students: Love what you do for a living. If one-third of your life involves work, make it your mission to find a job that you are passionate about. You will come home in a good mood. You will sleep well at night, and you will thrive in an environment that you enjoy being a part of every day.

Now that we have armed you with all this knowledge all we want is one thing from you. Please share what you have learned with others. Tell your friends, family, people that you associate with, just how rewarding a good reputation can be.

A lot of parents, after having children say, "I wish they came with a handbook." We would like to think this is a handbook that provides you with knowledge that may help you avoid disastrous situations in life. By deliberately and intentionally looking within and taking steps to truly become the person you are proud to be, you are on your way to creating your own *Reputation by Design*.

Reference

Skills gap? What skills gap? (n.d.). Retrieved from https://www.kornferry.com/institute/skills-gap-what-skills-gap

Index

A

ABCD method, repairing of reputation and, 63–64
Accountability, 97
Active listening, 81–82
Anxiety, 46
Appearance, 12–13
Attitude, 13–16
Authenticity
  core of, 7
  reputation and, 5–7

B

Behavior, 12–13
Belief, core values and, 28–30

C

Cheating, effect of, 58
Communication, 85–86
  ABC's of, 85
  laziness and, 87
  social media and, 46–47
Consistency, 3–4
Core values, 28–30

D

Depression, social media and, 47–48

E

E-mail, 76, 81

F

Facebook, 47, 76
Fear and doubt, 97
Flexibility, success and, 97
Forgiveness, 23

G

Goal, success and, 95–104
Gossip, 4
Grammar, 85

I

Integrity, 7–8

L

Lying, effect of, 58

M

Money, reputation and, 1–2

N

Negativity bias, 19
Notes, 73–79
180-degree lifestyle change, 62

P

Passion, 69
People magnet, 3
Plan, goals and, 98–99
Positive person, 23
Positive reinforcement, 26
Posts, social media and, 40
Public speaking, 83–84

R

Reputation
  authenticity and, 5–7
  bad writing and, 84–85
  builders
    image and, 32
    social media and, 49
  destroyers, social media and, 49
  gossip and, 4
  money and, 1–2
  repairing of, 57–66
    activity for, 65
  value of, 1–10

S

Self-compassion, 25
Self-destructive, 24

Self-esteem, 25, 27–28
Self-image, 19–38
Seven seconds, 11–17
Sleep, social media and, 46
Social media, 39–56
   addiction of, 43–44
   children and, 44
   golden rule in, 40–41
   jobs and, 42–43
   privacy and, 42
Speaking, reputation and
   preparation for, 84
   successful, 82–83
Success
   formula for, 63–64
   goal and, 95–104

T
Thank you note, 74–77
Trust, 2
Twitter, 63

V
Volunteering, 68–69
Vulnerability, 6

W
Words, usage of, 23–24